Media in Ireland: Issues in Broadcasting

MEDIA IN IRELAND

ISSUES IN BROADCASTING

EDITED BY
Damien Kiberd

OPEN AIR

Set in Janson by
Paradigm DTP for
OPEN AIR
an imprint of Four Courts Press
Fumbally Lane, Dublin 8, Ireland
e-mail info@four-courts-press.ie
and in North America for
Four Courts Press, c/o ISBS,
5824 N.E. Hassalo Street, Portland
Oregon 97213, USA

A catalogue record for this title
is available from the British Library

ISBN   1-85182-624-6

Printed in Ireland
by Betaprint Ltd, Dublin

Contents

Preface

DAMIEN KIBERD

The first half of this book concerns the relationship between big money, rapidly changing technologies and the electronic mass media.

The concentration of ownership and influence in the media industry is being matched in many countries by increased diversity of choice for the consumer. The application of digital compression technology to current television distribution systems (cable and satellite) and to the powerful networks of telephony companies must result in continuous audience fragmentation, a far greater range of choices for consumers and the breaking down of the power of once great media institutions. A determinism attends the process which cannot be resisted.

Money plays a key role at each stage in the process. Those with big money control television distribution networks and own intellectual property (see Halligan, pages 59-66). Those with at least some money may purchase temporary access to content. In the process large swathes of public service broadcasting are being driven out of existence or forced to adapt in a way which makes them virtually indistinguishable from commercial broadcasters.

Canute might try to resist this process. We cannot. Neither may it be possible for television and radio companies of the future simultaneously to discharge a public service remit while continuing to meet successfully their obligations to stockholders, employees and customers. History tells us that those with clear goals survive and prosper while those with muddled ambitions fail. Perhaps we should face reality by allowing full, unambiguous commercial freedom to all our broadcasting organisations while using whatever public money is available to finance broadcasting to discharge a much more tightly defined public service remit. Perhaps this will satisfy the stylishly expressed concern of Moynes (see pages 47-58) to retain a social purpose within broadcasting companies while facing commercial realities in an open, unelitist way.

The book also alludes to the growing impossibility of controlling the electronic media. Banning advertising aimed at children—even across the whole of Europe (see O'Brien, pages 30-46)—might provide temporary social gains in a world where children spend 6.5 hours per day watching television screens, videos and computer screens. Technology will ensure that such regulation becomes futile in the longer term. There have always been people who—for good or bad reasons—wanted to provide you only with what is good for you (their choice, your consumption). The dialectic of modern media suggests control processes will become more or less redundant. Media owners and innovators will make their choices about what they seek to sell to you and the only power that will check them is the changing nature of consumer preference. The same dialectic is also a key factor in the erosion of the position of public service broadcasters.

If this preliminary analysis seems unduly bleak, please consider the following. Many of the world's greatest books were written by authors who sought nothing more than money or fame. The same applies to the creation of works of art or to the making of important films. The world's finest investigative journalism has been done by journalists working for profit-hungry corporations. Lee hails the achievements of probing and thorough financial journalism (see pages 67-82) but even he would admit that the existence of a public service remit in a broadcasting company is not a condition precedent to the performance of such worthwhile tasks. Similarly the rather diverse range of ethical concerns raised by Gorevan (pages 23-29) are perhaps even more relevant to journalists working under strong commercial pressures than they are to those who are given the time and space to develop a more reflective approach to their work.

In an idiosyncratic contribution Duffy (pages 95-102) also examines the relationship between money and the media. Characteristically he poses some hard questions for media owners, managers and journalists. Most are middle-class, tend to use loaded language (often unintentionally) and make issues surrounding poverty boring through the manner in which they are reported. All pursue readers, viewers and listeners relentlessly—but they are invariably middle-class readers, viewers and listeners. The views and needs of the poor are often misrepresented, even bizarrely in advertising and press releases.

So much for money. Four of the ten sections in this volume, presented at the Eighth Cleraun Media Conference (see pages 131-132), relate to the reportage of conflict and they do not paint a flattering picture either of journalists or of the methods employed by the media.

After centuries of imperialism one might imagine that the media in countries such as Britain, France and Italy might have a reasonable understanding of regional conflicts in Africa, the near-East and central Asia. Yet Garcin's (pages 83-88) tour of recent reporting shows a quite terrible picture of selectivity, inaccuracy, bias, laziness and, of course, almost total reliance on one side's version of a particular conflict. O'Kane (a young but veteran war reporter) is equally critical of media coverage of conflict (see pages 89-94). The pool system which she describes in such graphic terms (where journalists operate under the umbrella of handlers from various war ministries and armies) has been operating recently in Afghanistan. Media companies wanting to send reporters into conflict zones, independently of these pools, find they cannot get life insurance for reporters or photographers. O'Kane suggests that unlike their counterparts in previous generations, many of today's war reporters have no stomach for personal risk. Instead they clog up hotels in areas adjacent to the theatre of action, looking for special treatment from army press officers to give them a competitive edge or, failing that, engaging in what is known as water cooler journalism (that is, journalists interviewing each other around the water cooler).

Beattie's reports of reporting in Northern Ireland (pages 103-113) offer greater cause for hope, though again his descriptions of graphic and truthful reportage concerning the victims of punishment beatings struck a chord among the public largely because such victims had been ignored in the bulk of the Irish and British media. At least he was not hindered in this work, nor in his efforts to depict the true, human consequences of the Omagh atrocity. By contrast the journalists described by Miller (pages 114-129) were trying to get through a brick wall of half-truths, misleading statements and overt censorship by the State and its security apparatus. Bizarrely, the peace process has increased the number of instances in which officialdom seeks to suppress unwelcome information. As players in the thirty-year conflict begin to talk and to reminisce, it seems that the State will only approve of officially-sanctioned (vetted) memoirs or exposés produced by paramilitary informers.

Is there cause for journalists to be concerned about all of this? Obviously, and the concern should run deep. Doing something about it is another matter, especially in a business where the next deadline may be a matter of minutes away and where there is little time to stop and think. Read this book. Then stop and think.

Introduction

WILLIAM HUNT

Within the already wide field of broadcasting, this book's range of contributors and topics—they include Joe Duffy on social exclusion, George Lee on the National Irish Bank tax-avoidance investigation he conducted with Charlie Bird, Breda O'Brien on children's television, Ursula Halligan on public service versus commercial broadcasting, and Maggie O'Kane on war reporting from Bosnia and Chechnya—may at first seem to defy any unifying theme.

Considering that there are also two chapters on Northern Ireland's media, one covering the Omagh bombing and the phenomenon of 'punishment beatings', and the other the uncertain transition from 'war' to peace-process journalism; a chapter giving the French perspective on the media's role in 'humanitarian' military interventions; one giving an RTE executive's perspective of the Authority's public-service remit; and another investigating the alternative sources of broadcasting ethics—one might almost conclude that this volume's objective was intentionally to display the diversity of broadcasting.

That, of course, it does do. Each of these ten views of broadcasting is like an individual facet of a dragonfly's compound eye, picking out very precisely one particular piece of its world. How interesting then that, having been brought together, they should be found to focus on broadcasting ethics. Only one actually addresses ethics as its main subject and even then, only to ask whether the very idea of 'media ethics' makes sense while few of the others even use the word 'ethics', and many present us with no obvious ethical issue to resolve.

However, the centrality of ethics to the issues raised in these chapters is best demonstrated, perhaps unexpectedly, in Breda O'Brien's assessment of children's television. We come away from her chapter with a heightened sense of the power advertising exercises over children, how and why it does so, and can quickly see that this power is a feature not of advertising, but of the media *per se*. The next, rather uncomfortable, step is our realisation that the difference between the power that the media exercise over our children and over ourselves is only one of degree, and possibly not as great a degree as we should like to think.

And it is the media's power, of course, that is the reason for media ethics. Each of the chapters of this book provides its own insight into the interaction of power and ethics within the broadcasting industry. They may not, taken together, provide many definitive answers but it is perhaps enough, for the moment, to be reminded how important the questions are.

Patrick Gorevan asks the fundamental question: is 'media ethics' an oxymoron? His evidence for its existence lies in the survey he provides of controversies that are to be found over the way in which the media should regard their ethics and the means that should be employed to monitor adherence to them, and his extended discussion of the role and limitations of codes of ethics.

He proposes that media ethics and the great moral issues impacting on truth-telling, the nature of privacy, the individual's place in society are interrelated and act on one another, but that ethics are not derived from morals any more than morals are derived from ethics. He cites the example of a member of a bio-ethics commission who found that, despite the very different moral perspectives of its members, they generally found it very easy to reach agreement on what should be done in individual cases: to decide, in short, what was ethical.

He later discusses whether media ethics might be simply a matter of professional competence and concludes that it is not. Certainly, it is difficult to argue that a more moral broadcaster would necessarily be a more competent one, or a more competent one, more moral. There would be no need for such an argument, however, if we view morality and ethics as disconnected.

It is perhaps conventional to suppose that the ethics of a profession, such as journalism, arise through extracting from a broader morality those principles that apply to the tasks performed by members of the profession, and then fashioning that selection of principles, elaborating them where necessary, into a system of ethics that addresses the issues the profession faces, in much the same way that one might extract iron from its ore and then fashion it into an axe for a woodcutter. The ethics that an Irish broadcaster followed professionally would therefore derive from the moral principles broadly accepted in Irish society.

But what if the relationship between ethics and morals is more like that of an electron to the nucleus of its atom? A mutual, high-energy interdependence in which each influences the other, is suited to the other, but neither has caused the other to exist? If we need equate competence only with ethics and not with morality, then we might reach a more open conclusion on this question. Is ethics simply competence?

The essential ethical obligation of the media is to inform the public. The first five words of the Society of Professional Journalists' code serves as a good starting point: seek truth and report it. (The rest of the code is, in effect, elaboration and constraint.) Sheer competence clearly plays a role: a journalist would be pretty useless if he were unable to find the truth, unable to recognise it when he found it, or unable to convey it with any clarity once he had recognised it.

If he recognised his inability to seek truth and report it, then it would not be ethical for him to continue to pretend to try; nor would it be ethical for a superior who recognised this inability to permit him to continue in a position that required this competence. It is not, of course, just a question of mastering technical skills. It is not enough to be able to seek truth and report it, he actually has to do it, whether he likes the truth he has found or not. Even more difficult, an ethical journalist must be willing to seek truths that he does not want to find, and look just as hard for them as for the ones he does want to find.

This equivalence of ethics and competence is, of course, essentially tautological. We merely establish that an ethical journalist, like a competent one, does what he is supposed to do. The question of just what he is supposed to do and who, ultimately, will do the supposing remains open. Unfortunately, the elaborations and constraints that any code of media ethics contains are very much part of the practice of broadcast journalism; they also often conflict with each other.

Morality can reinforce ethics. Accepting the obligation to operate within the ethics of a profession is a moral commitment, and a strong personal morality can make adherence to the ethic in the face of a conflict with, say, commercial pressures more likely. Morality may, on the other hand, just as easily undermine ethics. Too strong a commitment to any morality may blind a journalist to an awkward truth or give him the moral licence to suppress it, overriding his professional ethic.

Breda O'Brien, in making the practical and ethical problems raised by child-directed advertising the centrepiece of her discussion of children's television, provides us with a metaphor that makes clear why robust ethics in broadcasting, and within the media more generally, is vital to society. In a broad survey of the ways in which television influences young people, she clearly establishes that it not only affects the values that they form, but also affects their ability to absorb content from other sources of information—including the classroom. Parents of under-12s will be grateful that she has chosen to conclude with some brief, commonsense advice on how families may re-establish some control over their children's use of the medium.

She reminds us that television marketing to children comprises more than conventional ad-breaks between children's programmes; it includes, as well, product placement and the still relatively recent Pokémon phenomenon: programmes created for children solely for the purpose of promoting the sale of a spiralling network of branded products. We instinctively understand that there is something of concern about all this.

Few parents have not had a child, in asking for some new toy, say 'but he said it will be fun', or worse, heard a disappointed child, having just extracted the first fifteen minutes of enjoyment from a new toy and realising that they will also be the last, say 'but she said it would be more fun than this.' The 'he' or 'she' will perhaps have been someone they believe they have come to know through television, and perhaps come to think of as being something like a friend; and they suppose that this person has given them disinterested advice.

What we may only half-know instinctively, Breda O'Brien establishes as a fact: advertising to children must be unethical. The core principle of advertising, enshrined world-wide in the industry's codes of practice, is that advertising must always be easily identifiable as advertising, and it is impossible for children to identify advertising as such because they don't know what it is. Most children are unable to distinguish between programmes and advertising until they are between 6 and 8, and not until the age of 10 have virtually all children developed this ability. Children, until they can make this distinction, are likely to interpret an ad as the disinterested advice of a trusted friend. On this basis Sweden, for example, has simply banned all advertising directed to children under 12.

Breda O'Brien leaves us with an unsettling ethical problem: how can the advertising industry routinely sanction an activity that under its own rules is clearly unethical? How can it be that the 'hottest demographic' in children's advertising is now the 0 to 3 age range, the segment with the least ability to understand what is being done to them? And how can the media that carry these advertisements reconcile doing so with their own ethical obligations?

This, in its own context, may already be quite enough for us to think about; but if we take the issues that Breda O'Brien has raised as a model for our relationship with the media more generally, it becomes clear that she has also given us a means of better understanding the role that ethics should be playing, whether it is or not.

It is not only children who do not understand advertising. How many adults, in going out to buy a pair of sports shoes, will not know which brand our favourite star athlete wears? And how many of us, as we choose a pair for ourselves, will be *fully* conscious that he wears that particular brand only because he is paid an enormous amount to do so? Not all of us. If none of us could either remember what brand he wore or forget why he was wearing them, then he would most certainly be paid nothing at all, and there would be no advertising campaigns built around his 'choice' in athletic footwear.

Advertising works and it works very well indeed. It is a £500 billion-a-year industry, and the manufacturers who pay the bills get back their half-trillion and much more from us, as consumers, year in and year out. Why do we accept this? We ourselves are paying to be convinced to want things, to buy things, to believe things. This really doesn't make sense.

Society, of course, accepts advertising because each of us imagines himself, perhaps uniquely, to be immune from it. Advertising only influences other people; *I* make my own choices; *I* am an exception. It pleases each of us to suppose that the cost of television is the license fee (and the cable charge, if we have cable) and that radio is free. The cost is much higher, and we are all paying our share, because advertising affects our behaviour; neither is the cost, as Breda O'Brien points out, limited to the financial cost alone.

Advertising is immensely powerful. Despite our knowing what it is intended to do, and our trying to treat it sceptically, it succeeds in influencing our beliefs and behaviour enough to more than pay for itself. For example, the *Irish Times*, like most broadsheets, derives more than half of its revenue from advertising. It costs me £1 to read it over my morning coffee, but it also costs the paper's advertisers more than £1 for me to read it. Their costs of advertising in the paper—in-house costs, agency fees, and the *Irish Times*' charges—are more per copy than the price the reader pays. It is worthwhile for the advertisers to pay over a pound to expose me to their messages; we know that their messages work: they must change my behaviour enough to get back what it costs them plus a return on their investment every day, or they would stop advertising, and they haven't.

If the advertising content of the media can influence us so effectively despite our lack of trust in it—indeed, often despite our attempts to ignore it—how much more influential must the non-advertising content be? The media's potential for influence over us must be immense if we judge by the one segment of its content, advertising, for which there is an open market and which would not exist if it did not succeed in changing attitudes and behaviour.

Just as each of us is pleased to think himself immune from the effects of advertising, so each of us believes himself immune from the power of the media generally to persuade. This is why propaganda works: because we think it doesn't. The Soviet Union supported innumerable wasteful and pointless enterprises, but *Pravda* wasn't one of them.

It is this immense power of the media—which is only hinted at by advertising's effectiveness—that demands the adherence to ethics by both media organisations and individual broadcasters. The media's power must be wedded to responsibility if the media is to assist 'society as a community sharing a search for goodness' in Patrick Gorevan's words; and media ethics serve as the marriage vow. If they act ethically, then the media will do what they are supposed to do, what society supposes them to be doing—and seek truth and report it; if they do not act ethically, then the media become an unaccountable and illegitimate power capable of shaping society to their own ends.

Adrian Moynes, in addressing the social purposes of broadcasting, explores the intersection of the media, power, and advertising with the aim of assessing whether the electronic media have, in fact, had the high degree of impact on our lives that is often claimed for them. He proposes that our lives have probably been changed less than we imagine, in what has been a more evolutionary than revolutionary process. The limitations of his thought-experiment—trying to imagine pre-television life through experiencing a novel of the period—become clear when we try also to imagine the future attempt of someone trying to think himself back into life in our television age by watching 'classic' television. In either case a major feature of life would be missing: characters in novels do not read novels and characters on television do not watch television. Adrian Moynes' doubts about a pre-television golden age in which we were more active and inter-active find some support here.

While acknowledging that the media are 'radically commercial', he argues persuasively that the social purposes of broadcasting arise directly from the democratic life of our community and cannot be left to market forces to deliver in response to piecemeal profit opportunities—any more than we could leave justice, policing and defence to market forces and still expect to have a democratic rather than a feudal society once they had done their work.

Ursula Halligan, on the other hand, in her comparison of public service and commercial broadcasting, argues not only that the social purposes of broadcasting can be left to the market, but that by and large they should be. She notes that traditional public service broadcasters have already become more commercial—and not, in the case of RTE, solely due to its reliance on a combination of advertising and licence fee revenue from its beginning—because of three fundamental changes:

- the growth of individualism and the greater awareness by the broadcasters' audience of their power as consumers,
- technological developments that greatly expand the options of individual consumers, and
- the creation—through a combination of decline in the 'nation state' itself, the growing assumption of a national character by the European Union, the growing importance of group identities not based on nationality, and the rise of global media conglomerates—of a 'trans-national' culture, which cannot logically be addressed by any single state's public service broadcaster.

She sees public service broadcasters already functioning as hybrids, unable to discharge fully either public service or commercial roles, and foresees their becoming entirely sterile hybrids as these trends intensify.

The difficulty is that, while this may be an excellent diagnosis—is it a good prescription? Most would agree with Adrian Moynes that among the things we need from broadcasting are 'reliable, impartial news and information; free debate; diverse cultural self-expression; minority language rights; and a sense of being connected to the life of the people watching and listening.'

If these are needs rather than mere desires, how are we to assure that they are met, particularly if the case against our being able to rely indefinitely on public service broadcasting is a valid one? Broadcasters, in any case, will only meet these needs if they are recognised as such and firmly incorporated into broadcasting ethics, and the organisations and individuals within the industry then live by them. Is it, in other words, necessary that society should own individual public service broadcasters; or is the issue more whether or not society 'owns' the ethics under which all broadcasters operate?

George Lee's thoughtful reflections, in the context of financial journalism's place in public service broadcasting, on three aspects of his career as a specialist financial and economic reporter for RTE illuminate aspects of the Moynes-Halligan debate over public service broadcasting. In the first of these, he relates the progress RTE made recently in bringing the Central Bank from the point where it virtually ignored the broadcast media to today, when the requirements of broadcast and print media are accommodated more or less equally—and both far better than they would have been decades ago. Few would contest his view that a basic understanding of the economy and an appreciation of the implications of the more important current economic developments are important for all of us, as citizens; and fewer still, his observation that the nature of television makes it a particularly challenging medium in which to convey the complex analysis that this generally requires. It is open to us to wonder, therefore, whether the efforts George Lee describes on the part of RTE to open the deliberations of the Central Bank to its broadcast audience would have been justified *commercially*, and whether they would have been pursued as vigorously by a commercial broadcaster.

The history of his now-famous collaboration with Charlie Bird on the National Irish Bank (NIB) tax-avoidance investigation, which indirectly led to the DIRT (Deposit Income Retention Tax) inquiry, appears to fall even more firmly into a class of journalism that only a public service broadcaster could have undertaken. Their joint investigation was highly complex, time-consuming, initially not very promising in terms of clear results, and was always going to be risky (as the subsequent libel action established). In the event, the result was journalism of which all who contributed to it could be proud, and for which the public must be grateful; but it did not result, and could never have resulted, in very good *television*. A man with a microphone standing in front of a bank isn't good television unless the bank is literally on fire; NIB only burned figuratively.

Could a commercial broadcaster serving a market as small as the Irish one have justified the investment RTE made in the NIB investigation? Even if it were so, is it necessary that the broadcast media be prepared to take on the sort of investigations for which the print media are frankly better suited? Arguably, it is essential that broadcasters at least have the capacity to do so. After all, what if the issue requiring investigation concerned the print media itself—an abuse of market concentration, for example—and broadcasters were the only media clearly independent and unbiased?

George Lee's final issue, the controversy that resulted from his having characterised aspects of the government's Budget 2000 as 'Thatcherite', is a welcome reminder that public service broadcasting is no guarantee of lack of bias. There was nothing wrong with the characterisation itself, of course, and George Lee is right to stand over it. As he points out, television viciously time-constrains analysis, and demands that a reporter be able to convey the essence of his analysis in a pithy summary. The potential for bias reveals itself not in his comment, but in the controversy it sparked. George Lee seems to have been under the impression that Irish budgets were not supposed to be 'Thatcherite', and that to say one was constituted an attack rather than a description.

Thierry Garcin's analysis of the role of the media in setting the agenda in international humanitarian interventions, and the three chapters that follow it, remind us of the power of what might otherwise be regarded as an almost entirely innocent aspect of advertising—the simple provision of information. In four compelling case studies of our response to humanitarian disasters—in Iraq, Somalia, Rwanda, and Liberia—he assesses the role that the media played in forming the climate of opinion that ultimately determined the responses of western governments.

Perhaps most disturbing, he finds that the media have given little attention to the analytical background on which the fashion for 'humanitarian' military interventions rests, which means that the arguments advanced in favour of intervention in any particular case cannot be rigorously tested against generally-accepted criteria, because there aren't any. This lack of analysis allows the emotional impact of a disaster, which can be very effectively conveyed through the broadcast media, to predominate. Since the existence of a disaster alone is sufficient to demand a response, this also results in a tendency for journalists to simplify: to advance attractive but impossible solutions, to ignore complex background information, and to quickly identify heroes and villains.

Even more interesting, in many ways, is his evidence that it is the media who decide if and when a humanitarian disaster is occurring, or, in the words of Bernard Kouchner, 'There is no great disaster without large press coverage.' Thierry Garcin reminds us that the UN resolution authorising intervention on behalf of Iraq's Kurds applied equally to the Shiite Marsh Arabs, for whom virtually nothing was done. Because the Kurds were more accessible, more familiar to us already, or because their situation was that much more likely to be successfully resolved? Why was the war in Liberia and Sierra Leone ignored for so long? Why is the misery caused by the effective partition of the Congo by its neighbours the focus of so little attention? Why has the situation of Somalia, which is certainly no better than when its plight inspired the disastrous western military intervention of the early 1990s, dropped almost entirely from sight?

This ability of the media to select, from the range of events occurring in the world, those it wishes us to know about is, in many ways, its greatest source of power. We may at least hope to be alert to bias and framing in the news that is reported to us. The parallel, in advertising, would be that most of us know perfectly well that no product, regardless of the image its advertising attempts to project, is really going to change our lives.

Not all advertising is of this sort, however, and neither does the only risk of undue media influence arise from its ability to colour the information it gives us in order to persuade us to adopt the media's view. The media, simply by deciding which information we receive, have a tremendous power to direct belief and behaviour. Much advertising, too, works entirely on this basis.

Dixons, the electrical retailer group, for example, spend approximately £150 million each year, largely on print advertising. It mostly takes the form, not of any attempt to convince us that there is anything 'different, better and special' about Dixons, but almost entirely of lists of products available for sale at Dixons, and their prices. It is just information, and perfectly accurate information at that.

This is worth £150 million a year to Dixons because it is Dixons who select the information. They do not tell us what prices other retailers charge and they do not advise us what products are available in the market that Dixons do not sell. They are confident that, based on the information that they do give us, enough of us will visit them and buy something that they will more than get their money back. This is perhaps the media's greatest power because the very act of using it renders it invisible.

Thierry Garcin concludes that the recent approaches to humanitarian disasters taken by the media—sometimes careless and indiscriminate, not perhaps sufficiently thoughtful, often (especially in the broadcast media) driven by the 'urgency of urgency' felt by broadcasters themselves, and selected in some degree according to their susceptibility to effective televisual treatment—has contributed to an overload among the public. We are less interested and now less likely to give attention to interventions for which a powerful case could be made.

He does not see a refinement of broadcasting ethics or a revision of journalists' codes—which in France, at least, appear to be somewhat rudimentary—as the solution; but he proposes that what is essentially needed is that journalists use their common sense, which is not so very far, in fact, from invoking an ethics of competence.

Maggie O'Kane's selection from her ten years' experience in international reporting, with special emphasis on armed conflicts, suggests that one important factor governing which conflicts will be reported to us, and how, is the increased danger to journalists of this kind of work. She notes, for example, that the reason we hear so little of Chechnya is not that the conflict has abated, but that it is so bad that no major media organisation will send anyone in; and if you do not send reporters in, you do not get reports out.

She is deeply alarmed, as well, at the 'pool' system, first introduced in the

Falklands War and now a general practice among western military organisations. Partly in response to the dangers of conflict reporting and partly due to
the greater numbers of media organisations sending reporters 'in harm's way',
journalists are now expected to elect a few representatives whom the military
will then escort into conflict areas and who will then share their reports with
their colleagues. Clearly, by controlling where a very small group of reporters
go, the military can virtually guarantee what they will see; yet the appearance,
to the home audience, will suggest that hundreds of journalists have been
roaming freely.

This is perhaps the worst sort of 'Dixons effect': it is not even the media who
are selecting the information we receive, but one of the parties being reported
on.

Joe Duffy, in looking at the relationship between the media and social exclusion, is interested in a different sort of selection engaged in by the media. He
notes that speech radio appeals more to audiences higher on the socio-economic spectrum—RTE Radio 1, for example, having nearly twice the relative
appeal among the ABC1 segment as among the C2DE—and fears that this
reflects an orientation on the part of broadcasters rather than an inherently
lower audience interest at the C2DE level. He also suspects that in addition to
the obvious commercial appeal of the higher demographic, the middle-class
status of broadcasters themselves may play a role in this.

He argues that broadcasters select against coverage of issues and events that
would be of interest especially to the less well-off and the socially excluded, and
that exclusion may be reinforced by an unconscious identification with the middle class and a middle-class view of institutions. He proposes that journalists
must begin to interrogate the media itself and their fellow journalists on their
intentions and effectiveness in this area in exactly the same way that they interrogate other powerful institutions—now that journalists have perhaps become
'the most powerful group in Irish society.'

Michael Beattie—in featuring his own *Insight* documentary on 'punishment
beatings' within a discussion of the media's appetite for violence, brutality and
suffering—provides a most striking example of the media's power to select. He
notes that the media generally justify their description as 'a single black cloud'
that will 'travel anywhere ... to seek out any form of violence', but had largely
managed to ignore this particular form of brutality and the suffering it brought
to Northern Ireland, until *Insight* addressed the issue in 1999.

It was not that the black cloud's 'radar' had failed to register 'punishment
beatings'. Since the ceasefires they had increased in viciousness, frequency and
fatal outcomes; it was also clear that they were not an undesirable but almost
understandable form of vigilantism, but purely a means of maintaining local
pseudomilitary power. Also, they were happening at home. There was no need
to travel to some distant third-world battlefield to feed on violence; one could

have reached it in a van. Yet these attacks received from the media, before Michael Beattie's intense and powerful documentary, scant attention individually and little serious analysis as a phenomenon.

While an investigation of 'punishment beatings' would clearly require a degree of courage (the attribution of which Michael Beattie modestly declines to accept in his own case), the risks of opening this subject would have played only a small, if any, part in deterring the media. Clearly, the media suppressed its normal appetite for violence in favour of enhancing the chances of success for the peace process. In doing so, they imposed their own view, their own analysis—rather than making it clear to society what was happening and leaving it up to society to decide how to proceed.

Clearly, it would have been better for the peace process if 'punishment beatings' had not been occurring. Most of us had understood that honouring a 'ceasefire' would mean that the killing and maiming would actually end altogether. Unfortunately, 'punishment beatings' were occurring, and the media seemed to have decided that the next best thing was to act, insofar as possible, as if they were not.

David Miller surveys Northern Ireland's transition, following the Good Friday Agreement, to a peace-process media environment—without, curiously, any reference at all to the lack of attention to 'punishment beatings'. He discusses the adjustment to the end of the government broadcasting ban, the role of the Northern Ireland Information Service, evolving media priorities and coverage, and finally makes some suggestions on how the transition might be completed. Many of the examples he gives in support of individual points also serve to remind us of just how unusual is the media environment of Northern Ireland.

Journalists are routinely encouraged to be objective, and in most societies and on most topics something like objectivity can at least be approached. In the society of which he writes, however, given the events of the past thirty years, it quickly becomes clear that it is perhaps impossible to ask any individual, inside or outside the media, to 'be objective' with the expectation that he can do more than try to be so. Northern Ireland should perhaps serve to remind us that it is not so much objectivity as, overall, a balanced view that the public demand from the media and which the media are ethically obliged to deliver.

The ten chapters of this book—each representing a facet of the dragonfly's eye that comprises the whole—provides its own insight into an aspect of broadcasting that is of special interest to its author. In addition to increasing our understanding in its particular area, each can also be read as contributing to a broader appreciation of the power of the broadcasting media and the consequent importance of ethics in the exercise of that power.

Is 'media ethics' an oxymoron?

PATRICK GOREVAN

If 'media ethics' is an oxymoron it is a very busy one: a recent publication on media ethics entitled *Controversies in Media Ethics*[1] lists up to 18 different areas of controversy which are part of the province of communications ethics: freedom of expression, codes of ethics, manipulation of stories and the importance and possibility of objective accuracy, the public relations factor, the notion of correctness and inclusiveness, the clash between private lives and public interests, violence and sexual pornography, the role of the marketplace in keeping the media moral, infotainment, does ethics apply to advertising, how can journalists avoid conflicts of interest.

Those are some of the issues that arise from day to day: at a deeper level, we have the contrast, which has recently been aired in the United States, between *communitarian* and *individualist* journalism. Claude-Jean Bertrand has offered a pen picture of both which is hard to beat:

> Consider the following affirmations: mankind could not survive without solidarity; both the individual and the community matter; communication is essential to human nature; the mission of the media is to provide the public with a means of communication; whatever the media do that may jeopardise the persistence of mankind is unethical, evil. To a European at least, such statements are so obviously true as to look a little silly when strung together.
> *And, the alternative viewpoint,*
> human beings are isolated individuals whose rights and appetites are paramount; society should be ruled only by the forces of the market; media are nothing but businesses addressing customers; newspeople know very well what the public needs and wants; journalists' efficiency should be measured in pounds, shillings, and pence. Ethics, consequently, is often scorned as the icing on the cake.[2]

In this chapter, I claim that media ethics, far from being an oxymoron, holds a mirror up to human nature and touches on many of the key areas of morality

1 A. David Gordon and John Kitross (ed.), *Controversies in Media Ethics* (Longman, NY, 1998).
2 Foreword to C. Christians, J. Ferré, P. Fackler, *Good News. Social Ethics and the Press* (Oxford, 1993), vi.

tout court: the relationship of the individual to the community; private and public spheres; the nature of truth in human relations; the role of law and regulation in moral matters.

Media ethics and 'applied ethics'

Much work on media ethics is done from the standpoint of 'applied ethics'.
Alasdair MacIntyre, author of *After Virtue* and a foremost re-discoverer of practical ethics based on virtue, claims that the notion of 'applied ethics' rests on
the mistake of seeing ethics in rationalist way, as a set of timelessly valid principles, which are 'applied' to the passing flux of life.[3] This, for him, is the true
oxymoron. For MacIntyre, there is only 'ethics', and it is to be found precisely
in the passing and socially detemined situations of life, as we do our best to
deal with them. Timeless principles are not the place to start.

He offers an example in the work of an early commission on bio-ethics, a
thorny matter, by any standards: Stephen Toulmin, the philosopher, was a staff
member, and he reported that they differed profoundly on matters of general
moral principle, but still found it relatively easy to reach agreement on particular concrete issues, suggesting that what was happening could not properly be
termed 'applied ethics' at all.

What we call 'applied ethics' is simply ethics in action. There is no such
thing as a ready-made series of ethical principles, which then get applied to
'real life'. We only find ethical principles there, *in* real life: at the wheel of a car,
filling out our tax return, telling someone the truth. Media ethics is not an ethical backwater, or an application of some general principles. It is always re-open-
ing the discussion on the big moral issues: truth telling, the nature of privacy,
the place of the individual with regard to society, issues which the great moral
thinkers from Aristotle through Kant were engaged in.

Ethics as apprenticeship

This continuing ethical conversation works in many ways but for most people it
happens by a process of apprenticeship. Tom Wolfe's novel *A Man in Full*[4]
offers an interesting example of this. The turning point in Conrad Hensley's
journey from despair to redemption in prison comes when he is sent, in error,
not the spy thriller he had ordered (*The Stoics' Game*, by Lucius Tombs), but
The Stoics, the complete extant writings of Epictetus. Tedious stuff indeed,
about mysteries of life and the universe. But it was a book, and a
detail soon caught his attention. Epictetus had spent time in prison as a young
man. He had been tortured and crippled (as Conrad, too, expected to be) but
had ended up as one of the greatest Roman philosophers. Conrad had a sudden
overwhelming thirst for the words of this man. Epictetus began with the

---

3 Alasdaire MacIntyre, 'Does Applied Ethics Rest on a Mistake?' in *The Monist*, 67 (1984),
498–513. 4 Tom Wolfe, *A Man in Full* (Picador, London, 1999).

assumption that life is hard, brutal, punishing, narrow and confining, a deadly business, and that fairness and unfairness are beside the point. Epictetus had been there, and he had found a way of making sense of it. Now Conrad knows that he can too. He learns the lesson. He just has to look at things (and himself) as they are. He reads the story of Florus, who was asked (under pain of death) to take part in one of Nero's degrading plays and who goes to Agrippinus, the Stoic, and asks him what he should do. Agrippinus says 'You too? I was asked as well. I won't be taking part, but I think you should.' 'Why?' 'Because you considered it.' Once the thought had crossed your mind, well, that tells you *what you're like* and, as a Stoic, you must just accept that, even though you know that it is not the best thing to do.

Conrad has now become an apprentice in being an ethical human being. He isn't the first prisoner, the first who had to deal with the horrible situation he is in; there is a tradition in the practice of keeping up one's human dignity and, he feels, it might be worth seeing how the Stoics' approach might help him in his own situation.

The enterprise of ethical thinking makes us all apprentices who enter into the traditions of a practice, dialogue with Epictetus, Aristotle, Kant and Mill, and, as a result, make our own contribution to the practice's values and standards. Our greatest originality will often be that of appropriating the best, what we admire of those who have gone before us, and this applies both to journalism and to its ethics.

But it has to be the *best*. Apprenticeship can cut both ways and John Horgan has had harsh words for the less noble skills which can be picked up at work by journalists: 'water-cooler journalism', the tendency of journalists to agree privately among themselves what 'the story' was; how to second-guess their employers' and superiors' policies and prejudices, which would be useful in advancing themselves; how to use 'weasel words' to slant their reports against soft targets. For Horgan, there are many things Irish journalists learn on the job that they should not be learning.[5]

Is media ethics simply a matter of professional competence?

Douglas Birkhead, an ethics professor, recently asked his journalism students to write an essay on whether ethics, for a journalist, simply boils down to professional competence.[6] At first sight it is a compelling connection: incompetence is a form of moral failure, and developing one's talents appears to be a moral duty. But the students were not completely convinced: why should a competent person be regarded as a more moral one? Surely morality shouldn't depend on mastering technical skills? Others insisted that competence actually

5 *Irish Times*, 24 June 1999. 6 Douglas Birkhead, 'Should Professional Competence Be Taught as Ethical?' in *Journal of Mass Media Ethics*, 12 (1997) pp. 211–20 (esp. pp. 214–15).

depends on some basic moral precepts. He gave the highest mark to a student who said that some moral paradoxes are better left unsolved.

There are extreme positions here: some insist that great art and great journalism don't at all depend on the morality of the artist or journalist. Like Faust, many are ready to bargain a little morality for the sake of a good story or equivalent. Graham Greene recalled an event in hospital:

> There is a splinter of ice in the heart of a writer. I watched and listened [a heart-rending scene in the ward—all the other patients deliberately put on their earphones, full volume]. This was something I might need.[7]

Neil Jordan's film, *The End of the Affair*, is based on a novel in which Greene notoriously drew on his own and his lover's family's private lives. The message seems to be that writers inhabit a world of their own in which main-stream ethics do not apply.

Media ethics, I believe, cannot be reduced to media techniques; it needs more moral space than that. In fact it probably takes a whole society to be able to judge the morality or otherwise of what media professionals do, and the more ethical the system the wider the participation in ethical judgement and decisions. Morality operates through the journalist, agent of action, but also through the receptive activity of the conscientious reader, listener or viewer. Iris Murdoch wrote of the ethics of 'giving proper attention to things'. In schools here we have recently begun to help people to be critical recipients of mass media, and I believe it is a small but significant step. Our debate here in Ireland about guidelines, ethical codes and regulation of the media can best be understood in the light of this view of society as a community sharing a search for goodness.

Codes of ethics: a case in point

Conor Brady has explained that as a *quid pro quo* for the long-desired changes in libel laws, there might be an expectation that the print media would accept a press council or ombudsman.[8] Some newspapers, during the lobbying for a change in publishing law in the late 80s and early 90s, did get a Readers' Representative going, though this has since fallen by the wayside in many cases. But Brady didn't seem opposed to the idea of some kind of *self-regulation* regardless of whether the libel laws get reformed, even though a press ombudsman, he felt, would be a kind of culture-shock for Irish editors and journalists.

---

7 From *A Sort of Life*, quoted in Norman Sherry, *The Life of Graham Greene. Volume One* 1904–1939 (Penguin, London, 1990), p.323. 8 'Newspapers, Standards and Litigation', Damien Kiberd (ed,) in, *Media in Ireland: the search for ethical journalism* (Open Air, Dublin, 1999).

The NUJ, for their part, have supported the idea of a self-regulating press council.

Codes of Ethics: the argument in favour   Robert Pinker of the British Press Complaints Commission, speaking at the 1998 Cleraun Conference, claimed that the British system, with a code monitored by the Press Complaints Commission, works because:

> The Code belongs to the industry. The Code Committee consists of a small group of editors who have kept the Code under continuous review since they first wrote and circulated it to the industry for endorsement. All changes in the Code, whether they are major or minor in character, are made subject to the approval and support of the industry. Their compliance is voluntary but, nevertheless, it is binding. And that, in essence, is the strength of the self-regulatory system. Secondly, the industry has a manifest interest in making self-regulation work. If it were to fail, they know that the government would intervene and impose a statutory system.[9]

Cardinal Cahal Daly has claimed that there is a need for some kind of media ethics and standards council in this country. 'Every broadcast is a moral act', he said. It was therefore all the more necessary that there be 'voluntary agreement by the media themselves on the adoption of an ethical code of journalistic and media practice'.

In an ideal world that would be sufficient to prevent abuses, he said, but in the real world something more was needed 'in the way of some kind of media ethics and standards council, whose rulings would be made public, and which would have the power to investigate complaints and whose findings would be given some degree of binding force.'

Calling for more self-criticism within the media, he said that 'at present, it would seem that every institution in Ireland is subject to judgement by the media, except the media themselves.' Judgement of one's peers, he felt, was usually the most effective, as well as generally the fairest form of judgement.[10]

The Law Reform Commission's report (1998) on privacy concerned itself with the high-tech world of surveillance and how it should be regulated to protect the individual's privacy. The report proposed changes in both criminal and civil law to take account of the technology which, for example, allows a listening device to be concealed in a laminated business card.

9 'Can codes of conduct work?', in Kiberd (ed.), *Media in Ireland: the search for ethical journalism*, p.81. 10 *Irish Times*, 5 July 1997.

The Commission explicitly excluded self-regulation by the media, saying that they should be subject to the same legal controls as the rest of the public when it came to surveillance and improper disclosure of information. There would be a 'public interest' defence which could be invoked by the media, for example in the detection or prevention of serious crime, or the exposure of illegalities.

Finally, Senator Kathleen O'Meara has suggested 'a voluntary body organised and funded by the industry but with a very strong representation from the public, and in particular the socially excluded'. It should be chaired by a respected public figure, to help to give it credibility. Press councils should have two functions: to defend media freedom, and to improve the services the media offer. According to Breda O'Brien, if we establish a council, it should also look at issues such as concentration of ownership and near-monopoly of the media.[11]

Codes and Councils—dissenting voices   Codes of ethics are not an easy genre to write. The Society of Professional Journalists (SPJ) in the US published a 271-page handbook to accompany its three-page *Code of Ethics*. Small wonder that Charles Seib, former managing editor of the *Washington Star* and ombudsman for the *Washington Post*, could say that he had never seen an editor turn to a code or set of rules for guidance when faced with a real ethical call.[12] He also remarked, however, that 'whenever three or more newspaper editors meet, it is hard to stop them drafting a code of ethics.'

John Merrill, a media ethics academic writing from an individualist stance, rather suspicious of regulation, claims in a recent written debate[13] that a main problem with most codes of ethics is that they try to do too many things at once. Their writers are never sure whether to make them *inspirational* (credal) or *normative* (legalistic). The SPJ code deals with freedom of the press, calling on journalists to guard it, but failing to note that it is just this freedom that calls into play many *unethical* practices which the SPJ code writers would condemn.

David Gordon, in a contribution to the same debate, rejects criticism aimed at the inherent ambiguity and awkwardness of codes of ethics. He believes that they have to be both absolute and relative and what is wrong with that? Are they lofty rhetoric? What is wrong with that either? Ethics by its nature deals with what *should* happen rather than what can be legally enforced.[14]

It is tempting to regard journalism as parallel to medicine, in which practitioners may be struck off the register for unsuitable behaviour. There are differences, however. Alleged medical malpractice, for example, rarely has political dimensions, but supposed wrongdoing by a journalist often does. This may leave the journalist and even the statutory body open to political pressures to 'do something'. At least a few fail-safe mechanisms will be needed in this area.

11 Breda O'Brien, *Sunday Business Post*, 2 August 1998. 12 Gordon and John Kitross (ed.), in *Controversies in Media Ethics*, p. 61. 13 Ibid., p. 68. 14 Ibid., p. 64.

The objection is also made that harm caused by media reporting is not on the same scale as the damage caused by medical malpractice. It does not require much imagination to see that at times it is: a report may cause immense distress and invasion of privacy, even threats to life.[15]

For Michael Foley, many of the examples quite properly cited as proof of falling standards (invasions of privacy or grief, stereotyping of minorities or nationals, money being paid to witnesses) could not be dealt with by the quasi-judicial process that a press council implies—not without interfering with freedom of expression. Rather than add another layer of regulation, to be administered by a press council, he felt it might be time to loosen control of the press and at the same time address ethical questions with a degree of subtlety.[16] Perhaps that ethical subtlety could be provided by in-service training for journalists and by the university media faculties. Without this broader moral awareness, codes of practice may turn out to be well-meaning phrases, ritually trotted out to show that all is well, this is an 'ethical' profession.

Conclusion

So, is media ethics an oxymoron? They say that people vote with their feet. So let me answer the question, in the negative, with a political anecdote. One of the strangest episodes in a very strange British General Election in 1997 was the election of Martin Bell, a journalist, running in Tatton on an anti-corruption ticket. Nobody laughed, or felt that the cure was going to be worse than the disease. Symbols mean everything and it was a journalist who symbolized people's anger at what had been going on. The electors of Tatton were not naive; many presumably felt that journalists, too, had a lot to answer for. But they voted Martin Bell in with some ease, and they knew what they were doing.

In Ireland we have not voted too many journalists into the Dáil as yet, but there is a strong sense of the profession as concerned with truth, with standards and not afraid of self-criticism. Like Florus, like ourselves, communicators look into the abyss and may well be tempted to take short cuts, to act as if no one were looking. But this is what ethics is all about: eternal vigilance not just on crime or on corruption, but also on oneself.

15 Nigel Harris, 'Codes of conduct for journalists' in A. Belsey and R. Chadwick, *Ethical Issues in Journalism and the Media* (Routledge, London, 1992), p. 68 (and see p. 9). 16 *Irish Times*, 23 February 1999.

Children and television—not just child's play

BREDA O'BRIEN

There is a terrible temptation to use television as a scapegoat for all our ills, whether it be teenage killers in the US or gruesome murders of toddlers nearer to home. Life is, of course, much more complicated than that, and television is part of a complex interaction of social factors.

While taking a brief look at other issues, my contention is that television has a significant influence on the formation of attitudes in young people, particularly in the area of values and the search for happiness. In other words, it is my contention that, unless it is used very carefully, much of television helps to produce consumers rather than thinkers. Television can be a potent training school for developing what is called 'consumer socialisation' in children. To that end, I concentrate on the role of advertising and the ethics of advertising to children, and on the positive use of television in educational programming. My focus is on children up to age twelve.

It may seem strange to be concentrating on television at a time when new media such as the internet dominate the headlines. However, if you will pardon the image, television acts like a portal site into many of the newer media and, in the future, will literally be such a portal. Since television is being revolutionised with the advent of digital television, now is a good time to look closely at what we want television to become, and what needs to be put in place to ensure those goals are met.

It is important to remember that there are potentially great benefits in the medium of television. Aletha Huston and John Wright, American researchers specialising in educational television for children, have this to say:

> Television can teach academic and social skills; it can help viewers to understand social issues, feelings, and perspectives; it can bring about understanding of ethnic diversity and reduce stereotyped attitudes, to name only a few domains. The visual character of television is a plus for most kinds of learning. It helps to engage children, and it offers them a mode of representation that complements and clarifies messages that are carried by language as well. Children can learn factual and conceptual information from television, and they can generalise

what they learn. By means of television, children can travel in time and space to the 'not here' and the 'not now'. Variations in pace and segment length can be carefully crafted to hold children's interest without leading to problems in attention span. Television does not necessarily displace more valuable activities; the effects of television on many aspects of learning are more a function of program structure and content than of the medium itself.[1]

All of this is true. However, Wright and Huston are speaking specifically about carefully designed educational television, not mindless dross. Many parents have a deep unease about the central role which television plays in children's lives. Likewise, many teachers report a drop in children's attention span and a greater assumption that they will be entertained, which educators attribute, rightly or wrongly, to the central position of television in the lives of children. There are issues as simple as: 'What would children be doing if they were not watching television?', the so-called displacement effect. Wright and Huston claim that when television first became prevalent in America, what it mostly displaced was other media, such as the radio.

The Nickelodeon channel actually seems quite proud of the fact that television displaces other activities. One of their promotional slots, used during 2000, showed empty playgrounds, parks and gardens. The slogan is 'Where is everybody?' The final shot was a house bulging with children—all indoors watching Nickelodeon.

Now that it is an established medium, there is no doubt that the hours spent in front of the television do actually prevent children doing many other things. The Annenberg Public Policy Center of the University of Pennsylvania conduct mammoth studies on television and computer usage in American homes. Their survey in 2000 showed that the time a child spent in front of the television, video recorder, computer and videos games amounted to an average of 6.5 hours a day. There is no reason to believe that Irish statistics would be very different.[2]

Anecdotal evidence would suggest that there has been a decline in traditional children's games. The American Academy of Pediatrics has highlighted excessive television viewing, and more importantly the sedentary lifestyle which accompanies it, as a factor in childhood diseases such as diabetes. In 1999 they went so far as to say that children under two should not watch television at all, and that television for older children should be severely restricted, to one or

1 Aletha C. Huston and John C. Wright, 'Television and the informational and educational needs of children', in *Annals of the American Academy of Political and Social Science*, 557, May 1998, p. 19.
2 Emory H.Woodward, Natalia Gridina, *Media in the Home 2000: The Fifth Annual Survey of Parents and Children*, Annenberg Public Policy Center at the University of Pennsylvania: *www.appcpenn.org/mediainhome/survey*

two hours a day. 'No reliable research has been done on how television viewing affects children younger than two', Dr Marjorie Hogan, the lead author of the report, said. But the academy based its recommendations for such children on knowledge of what babies need for proper brain development—notably close-up interaction with older people—and the common-sense notion that if they are watching television, babies are not getting those other essential stimuli.[3]

Intriguingly, the authors of the report also recommend that doctors take a media history of their young patients, and provide sample questions to ask. They also heavily recommend that children should not have television sets in their bedrooms and that television viewing should be limited to one to two hours a day for older children. The Annenberg study shows that this is extremely unlikely to happen.

This is disturbing on a number of counts. One of the issues, which have been well researched, is the effect which televised violence has on children. This has been extensively researched, not surprisingly perhaps, in the United States, where high-school-age killings have sadly become almost commonplace. In the United States it is accepted among researchers that there is not a direct cause-and-effect relationship between acts of violence and viewing violence. It is obviously much more complex than that. Dubow and Miller state:

> Most of the evidence from laboratory, observational, and cross-cultural longitudinal studies indicates that violence in television and other media plays a causal role in the development of aggression. Most researchers acknowledge that television violence viewing is only one of many causes of aggression (other causes include family environment characteristics), but conclude that it is nevertheless of social significance.[4]

It is generally accepted that repeated exposure to television violence has a desensitising effect. Likewise, it can lead people to what George Gerbner called the 'mean and angry world' effect, to feel that the world is a darker place than it actually is, and that people are not to be trusted. That this is accepted in the United States is not surprising, given the following statistics from the Centre for Media Education in Washington:

> By the time children complete elementary school, the average child will witness more than 100,000 acts of violence on television, including 8,000 murders. These numbers double to 200,000 acts of violence and murders by the time they graduate from high school. Prime-time tele-

---

3 Lawrie Mifflin, 'Pediatrics Group Offers Tough Rules for Television', *New York Times*, 4 August 1999. 4 Eric F. Dubow, Laurie S. Miller, 'Television Violence Viewing and Aggressive Behaviour', in *Tuning in to Young Viewers—Social Science Perspectives on Television*, Tannis MacBeth (ed.), (CA 1996, Sage Publications), p. 142.

vision contains about 5 violent acts per hour compared to an average of 26 violent acts per hour during Saturday morning children's television.

Though the research concludes, in relation to aggression, that television violence viewing is only one factor, it is nevertheless a socially significant one. If we accept that it is true in one area, at the very least it points towards the likelihood that television can have a socially significant effect in other areas also. This is not to say that all viewers, at all times, will be influenced in the same way. But neither is it to say that there are not times when most viewers will in fact receive the same message.

Most researchers agree that children comprise a 'special audience' for television. As Dorr (1986) points out, children's limited knowledge of the larger world has several implications for their transactions with television: they may fail to understand or may misunderstand programme content if they lack the necessary background knowledge; they may accept television content as accurate information when other more knowledgeable viewers know it to be otherwise; and they may evaluate content without considering the means and motives for broadcasting it.[5]

All of this has obvious implications for the question of advertising. We are inclined to see advertising as a kind of 'add-on', which is a naive attitude. Except where massive public funding is poured into broadcasting, advertising is not some kind of add-on to television, but an absolutely central plank. This is true of many other media also. As Colm Rapple pointed out to the Sixth Cleraun Media Conference in 1996, 67% of the revenue of the paper for which he used to write, the *Sunday Business Post*, came from advertising.[6]

I believe that the central question is not just the individual advertisements themselves. In the case of children, to be more concrete, it is not just a question whether certain children pester certain parents for certain products at particular times of the year, but whether the constant presence of advertising relays a message almost subliminally to children. This message might be summed up as saying that all human beings are lacking in certain ways, and that the possession of certain attributes, products or services will bring about happiness. In other words, does the constant presence of advertising influence children in the direction of becoming happy little compliant consumers?

An article on China in the *Journal of Consumer Marketing* sheds some interesting light on this question. China has embraced elements of the market economy, and its enormous population makes it a very enticing market for all sorts of businesses. Television as a mass medium is a relatively recent arrival also. China is particularly interesting for marketers because branding and advertising

5 A. Dorr, 'Television and Children: A Special Medium for a Special Audience', (1986), (Newbury Park, CA, Sage), p. 13, quoted in *Tuning in to Young Viewers*. 6 Damien Kiberd (ed.), *Media in Ireland: the search for diversity* (Open Air, Dublin, 1997, p. 70).

are relatively new concepts there. As the author explains, one has to learn to be a consumer:

> Children must know about products, their attributes and their benefits, in order to form attitudes toward them, desire them, and make purchase decisions about them or ask their parents to purchase them. In developing countries like China, where new marketing practices such as branding and advertising are appearing, children as well as their parents need to learn consumption-related behaviours in order to adapt to the changing conditions in the marketplace. Children learn their consumer-related skills, knowledge, and attitudes through interaction with various social agents in specific social settings, a process that is usually termed consumer socialization (Ward, 1974) or consumer development (McNeal, 1964).[7]

Obviously, the primary socialisation agent is the family. But the author acknowledges the influence of the mass media in teaching consumer behaviour:

> Thus the interactions between the mass media and the public—children and adults—are very important to marketing managers who, in effect, believe that what is prominent in the media becomes salient in the public's mind, and in turn produces consumer-related behaviours such as shopping and purchasing (Sutherland and Galloway, 1981; Wartella, 1981). This thinking is particularly important in the case of children where it is believed that many of the consumer attitudes and behaviours they develop will be applied throughout much of their lives (Guest, 1955; McNeal, 1987). A second party, their parents, may indirectly feel the impact of the mass media on children. Children who receive messages from the media may in turn convey these messages to their parents, perhaps in the form of requests for products. Finally, the amount of interaction with the media appears to be positively related to learning consumer behaviour. That is, the more that children interact with the mass media, the more consumer socialization takes place (Moschis and Churchill, 1978; Moschis and Moore, 1982; O'Guinn and Shrum, 1997).[8]

The phrase 'consumer socialisation' is fascinating. This author is quite open about the required outcome: that people, particularly children, should acquire a set of attitudes towards consumption which trains them in consumer behaviours. Of course, we all need to consume. The question is: what kind of con-

7 James U. McNeal, Mindy F. Ji, 'Chinese children as consumers: an analysis of their new product information sources', *Journal of Consumer Marketing*, 16:4 (1999). 8 Ibid.

sumption do we need? The simple lifestyle is not one that the free market has much time for:

> The findings suggest clearly that the television generation of China is here and now. The children regard it as an important new product information source more than any other medium, more than they do stores, and more than they do parents, grandparents, and friends—in a culture where the basic social unit is the family. *Obviously, television is having an emancipating effect on China's children* (emphasis mine). It is reducing their reliance on traditional interpersonal sources of product information while catering to their need for entertainment. Television's central informational role makes it the most likely candidate as a communications channel for domestic and international marketing managers looking to target the children of China as consumers.[9]

Note the identification of learning consumer behaviours with emancipation from family. The author has harsh words for those wimps and wets who might think that this might not be altogether desirable:

> There is a body of opinion that expresses concern (and even outrage) about the targeting of advertising at children. In Europe there is a persistent 'consumerist' lobby seeking to restrict or even ban such advertising. Elsewhere there are legal or self-regulatory constraints on advertising aimed at children. As marketers we must be aware of these issues and, in most cases, should prepare to defend the current position. In all developed society, the commercial message is an integral part of the culture. Advertising is not some kind of privilege granted to businesses but represents a fundamental element of the business process—as important to the consumer as it is to business.[10]

The training of children as consumers is well illustrated by two advertisements, both aired during children's programmes on RTE's *Den 2*. One is for 'L'Oreal Kids'—a shampoo aimed at children. It contains several key ingredients. It promotes brand loyalty on the grounds that if children begin to use a brand in early childhood they will stick with it into adulthood. This may be wishful thinking on the part of advertisers, but it is also based on research. Secondly, there is constant repetition of the brand name 'L'Oreal'. It encourages children to see themselves in adult terms by using the slogan: 'Because we're worth it, too'. The adult slogan is: 'Because I'm worth it'. Note the expectation that children will recognise the adult slogan, promoted by the likes of Claudia Schiffer and Jennifer Aniston.

9 Ibid. 10 Ibid.

The second is an advertisement for 'Nivea' anti-perspirant, featuring a mother and daughter in a scene of emotional closeness which revolves around playful use of the anti-perspirant by the child. It works on several levels: the woman who uses this anti-perspirant is a good mother, a good role model with a close relationship with her daughter. It is obviously primarily aimed at mothers, but there is an interesting sub-text for little girls watching: this is what it is to be a grown-up woman, this is what grown-up women do and buy. It exploits an age-old phenomenon similar to that which sees four-year-olds clacking along in mother's high heels and pretending to be grown-up. There are those who see nothing sinister in this marketing aimed at children, who claim that children are much more capable of negotiating and navigating the world of advertising than we give them credit for. This viewpoint would be quite dismissive of fears which parents would have, particularly regarding the encroachment on innocence. Chief among those in Britain who hold this view is Dr Brian Young. A flavour of what he believes can be gained from an article published in the *Irish Communications Review*. He finds the arguments of Kessen, an American child psychologist, persuasive. In 1979, Kessen wrote an article entitled 'The American child and other cultural inventions'. Kessen believes that the transition from 'a rural to an industrial economy in the nineteenth century resulted in far-reaching changes in the way people viewed the family and childhood':

> The world of commerce and industry was centred on the town. This was where men worked; this was where wheeling and eating, haggling, arguing, buying and selling and negotiation in smoke-filled saloons occurred. The world of commerce and industry was rough, tough, sinful and self-interested. In contrast, the world of the home—where men returned with a 'Hi, Honey, I'm home'—was romanticised and transformed into an idealised world of domestic bliss and motherly values. Childhood was sentimentalised. Children were to be protected from the decadence of downtown and to be a child was to be innocent and pure. *Later he adds*: What happens when the images of the defenceless child and the evil advertiser are put together? What does this produce? An image of the relationship between children and television where the child is seen as the innocent and the advertiser as seducer.[11]

Kessen believes that this view of innocent child and advertiser as seducer is too simplistic. Young also rejects it in favour of a vision of the child not as defenceless, but active: 'growing and developing an understanding of the economic and social world of which advertising and marketing is an important and inescapable fact'.[12]

11 Brian Young, 'Is Advertising to Children a Problem?', *Irish Communications Review*, 6, (1996). See also Brian Young, Marion Hetherington, 'The literature on advertising and children's food choice', *Nutrition & Food Science*, 5 (1996), pp. 15-18.

In short, Young does not feel children should be protected from advertising because learning to deal with it is a vital part of negotiating our culture. Yet Young's own research at the University of Exeter shows that children do not understand advertising until the age of four and do not clearly grasp the concepts till at least age eight, and many not until age ten. It is not until the age of 12 that their understanding of advertising can be said to be comparable to that of adults.

What about the marketers?

> Listen to Stephen Colegrave of Saatchi and Saatchi: 'Children are much easier to reach with advertising. They pick up on it fast and quite often we can exploit that relationship and get them pestering their parents.' Earlier this year, Saatchi sponsored a two-day conference on 'Marketing to Kids' with, to quote their brochure, 'an interactive workshop using real live children'.[13]

Kidscreen, a magazine geared towards marketing to children, said the following:

> Stripped down to basics, brands that work best satisfy a timeless emotional need, while being flexible enough to change with the times, according to Gene Del Vecchio, president and founder of youth consulting firm CoolWorks. Barbie, for example, satisfies a girl's need for glamour, and Mattel keeps it current by dressing Barbie up according to the times, be it as a stewardess or as an astronaut.[14]

Later in the same article:

> Advertising, accordingly, must address those twin concerns. Once agencies identify the aspect of a product that taps into a child's deeper motivation, they can structure messages that connect with kids on psychological and emotional levels, according to Anne Adriance, strategic planning director for Saatchi & Saatchi Kid Connection. 'Trix' cereal's tag line, 'Trix are for kids', reflects the core emotional concept of campaign: that 'Trix', literally, is made for kids. 'In a world where there's a lot that's not for kids, to create a whole product ... exclusively for [kids] gives children a sense of power, a sense of control and a sense of independence that they don't always have in their life,' she says.[15]

It's ironic that the appropriately named 'Trix' offers children 'a sense of

12 Helen Seaford, 'Should Our Children be spared Ronald?', *The Guardian*, 22 November 1999.
13 Ed Kirchdoerffer, 'Keeping Up with Today's Kids: Part One of a Three Part Series', *Kidscreen*, January 1999, p. 41: *www.kidscreen.com/articles/KS24101.asp* 14 Ibid. 15 Ibid.

power, a sense of control and a sense of independence', all by suckering them into buying a particular brand. And it is no coincidence that one of Nick-elodeon's television slots, *Nick Junior*, which is geared towards the youngest viewers, repeats *ad nauseam* the slogan, 'Just for me'.

Kidscreen also informs us that:

> Agencies are cautiously eyeing the zero-to-three demographic, a group that poses tremendous challenges and opportunities because research has indicated that children are capable of understanding brands at very young ages. 'Traditionally, it's been a parent target, but we're going to see that change in a big way,' says Paul Kurnit, president of Griffin Bacal. 'We've been seeing it in programming [*Barney, Teletubbies*]; it's just a matter of time before we see it in advertising as well.'[16]

In its 1999 survey (15), the Annenberg Public Policy Center (mentioned earlier) questioned US parents and 10-17 year-olds about children's programme-related activity and the use of programme-related products. According to parents, their children were most likely to ask for programme-related toys (32.9%), read books based on television programmes (28.6%) and play games based on shows (24.6%). In addition, 17.5% of their children had read maga-zines based on programmes, 15.2% had visited web sites and 11.4% had used a CD-ROM based on a show: see Figure 1.

Children's desire for and use of programme-related products changed as the child got older. Elementary (6-11) and secondary-school-age young people (12-17) were more likely to visit web sites based on television programmes and read magazines based on shows. As children grow older, they were less likely to play games, ask for toys, read books or use CD-ROMs based on television programmes: see Figure 2.

So in this Annenberg survey, 62.1% of children from ages two to five asked for a toy related to a programme in the month prior to the survey. A most interesting aspect is that all such activity is strongest in the under-fives.

Psychologists like Dr Brian Young may not see this as problematic, but a group of sixty psychologists asked the American Psychological Association (APA) to stop the abuse of psychology and to censure those who profit by sell-ing information on child development to advertising agencies:

16 Jeffrey D. Stanger, Natalia Gridina, *Media in the Home 1999: The Fourth Annual Survey of Parents and Children*, Annenberg Public Policy Center at the University of Pennsylvania: *www.appcpenn.org/mediainhome/survey*

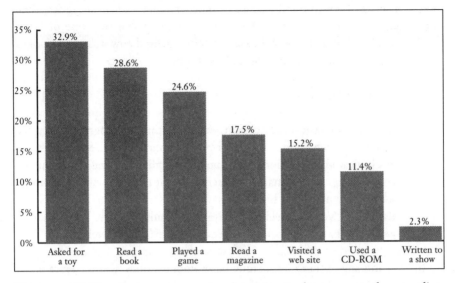

Figure 1: Children's programme-related activity in the past month, according to parents

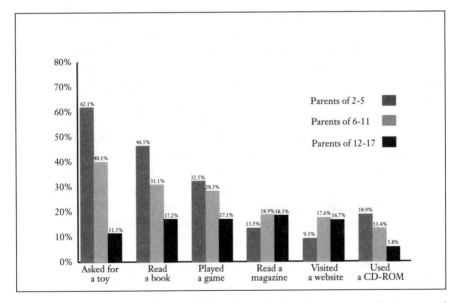

Figure 2: Children's programme-related activity in the past month, by age of child, according to parents

Specifically, we urge the APA to:

(1) Issue a formal public statement denouncing the use of psychological techniques to assist corporate marketing and advertising to children; and,

(2) Amend the APA's Ethics Code to establish limits for psychologists regarding the use of psychological knowledge or techniques to observe, study, manipulate, harm, exploit, mislead, trick or deceive children for commercial purposes; and,

(3) Launch an ongoing campaign to probe, review and confront the use of psychological research in advertising and marketing to children. The campaign would include:

(a) ongoing investigation of the use of the tools of psychology in advertising, marketing and market research targeted at children;

(b) publication and ethical evaluation of these findings; and,

(c) the promotion of strategies to protect children against commercial manipulation and exploitation by psychologists and those who use the tools of psychology.

The use of psychological insight and methodology to bypass parents and influence the behaviour and desires of children is a crisis for the profession of psychology.[17]

So which is it? A crisis for the profession of psychology, or an inevitable part of life which children must come to terms with? The Swedes have come up with a clear answer, which is to ban advertising directed at children. Why?:

Because young children do not understand what advertising is. And according to the commercial community itself, they should. In the International Chamber of Commerce Code of Advertising Practice which is supposed to govern the industry's self-regulation all over the world, one basic principle concerns advertising identification: advertising should be easily identified as such. You will find corresponding language in various legal instruments, for instance the European Commission's 'Television without Frontiers Directive' and the Swedish Marketing Act.

This means that everybody in the target group should be able to distinguish easily an advertisement from other media content, and also understand the purpose of it. They should be able to do that in the context where the advertisement generally occurs, for example as part of a television broadcast. This is so important because it establishes a

17 Letter to American Psychological Association signed by sixty psychologists: *www.essential.org /
alert*

basic balance of power between the consumer and the advertiser. In other words it establishes the principle of fair play.[18]

This is a simple reason. Children who do not understand what is going on should not be the target of advertising, because it is not 'fair play'. A typical example of this is the 'Haribo' advertisement, which uses cartoon-style graphics to sell sweets. This cartoon style would be very difficult for a young child to distinguish from a programme.

Interestingly, the Swedish ombudsman quotes research very similar to Young's in order to bolster his case:

> In 1994, the Swedish sociologist Erling Bjurstrom published a comprehensive survey of international research on the effects of television commercials on children. He concluded that even if some children can distinguish between advertising and programmes as early as age 3 or 4, in most children this ability does not develop until the age of 6 to 8. And it is only by age 10 that practically all children have developed this ability.[19]

He also counters the argument that children must learn to live in this advertising-dominated world:

> It is true that measuring the awareness of young children is not an exact science. Children are different and so are social scientists. But I am convinced that most parents are perfectly well equipped to judge the needs of their children. They want to take responsibility themselves for bringing up their children. They would be likely to say 'no thank you' to any offer from the advertising industry to take over the media education of their children. I am also convinced that, if they would have a chance to choose, parents would opt for a television free from advertising targeted at children. At least this appears to be the case for Sweden.[20]

There obviously will be great opposition to such a move from advertising agencies because of the loss of revenue. RTE would doubtless also be nervous, even though it says that the revenue from children's advertising is quite insignificant. I cannot say for certain whether it is or not because, when I requested figures, I was told that it was 'commercially sensitive information'. In relation to the

---

18 Speech (London, 23 November 1999) regarding television advertising to children by Axel Edling, Director General of the Swedish Consumer Agency, and the Swedish Consumer Ombudsman: *http://www.essential.org/alert/television/Edlingspeech.html* **19** Ibid. **20** Ibid.

overall funding which RTE receives, approximately one third is from the licence fee and the rest is from advertising.

There is a persuasive case for getting the whole of the European Union to 'jump together'. Sweden wanted its presidency in 2001 to issue a ban on advertising to children. It would perhaps be unreasonable for RTE to do so unilaterally, but obviously it would be much easier to do so in the context of an EU-wide ban. The Swedish presidency was unable to achieve consensus on the move due in part to determined lobbying by advertising interests.

How does RTE do in relation to advertising? It has quite strict guidelines. No advertising is permitted during pre-school programmes, and during the rest of the time advertisements are roughly two advertising breaks per hour. So RTE has self-imposed guidelines, and the Broadcasting Commission of Ireland (BCI) guidelines, which are quite strict, also specifically outlaw 'pester power'.

There is an area, however, in which RTE falls down badly, which is in product placement. RTE continually offers the latest merchandise as prizes in competitions.

To show how adults can be 'product-blind' while children are being socialised into brand recognition at younger and younger ages, I showed a still taken from *The Den* to a group of over 100 adults at a seminar. The set for *The Den* at the time was dressed as a child's playroom with toys strewn all over the place. I asked the adults how many products they recognised. Very few, was the answer. The same experiment conducted with my seven-year-old son and one of his friends had them reeling off a list of branded products which finally totalled fourteen. These ranged from soft toys marketed as a promotion for the Cadbury chocolate 'Yowie' product, to *Sesame Street* characters, to Pokémon toys, and on and on. 'Socky', one of the puppet characters who present *The Den*, was even wearing a 'Thomas the Tank Engine' scarf. The subliminal message is that this is what 'cool' kids play with. There were almost no generic, non-branded toys. What looks like a colourful set to adults conveys an entirely different message to children.

RTE does show infomercials using the children's heroes in an attempt to balance out the mad emphasis on spending. But RTE is now 'head-to-head' with the Nickelodeon channel and, to be quite honest, the schedules are pretty indistinguishable. There is a huge overlap in the types of programme shown. Ironically, two of the better programmes from Nick Junior, *Blues Clues* and *Magic School Bus*, do not appear on the schedules in RTE. *Blues Clues* is a carefully-designed and award-winning pre-school programme, which utilises knowledge of children's developmental processes in order to stretch their logic and reasoning. *Magic School Bus* is a science-based programme for early-to-middle childhood, which is really excellent, particularly when taped and re-watched. Books of the series which expand on the science are the primary 'tie-in' merchandising.

A comparison between RTE's morning schedules in 2000 and 1999 provided interesting results. RTE dropped its *Open Learning* slot which contained educational programmes for about an hour and a half. Some were designed for school use, but there were also excellent programmes such as *Muzzy*, an Irish-language learning programme which pre-schoolers loved. The type of programming that predominated in 2000 was almost indistinguishable from Nickelodeon.

Until the announcement about its digital channels, RTE was never committed to educational television in the first place, and its current scheduling shows no commitment or, to be honest, much understanding of the idea of educational television. It now broadcasts some of these educational programmes at five o'clock in the morning, but they appear at the end of the previous day's schedules because the broadcasting day begins at six o'clock. So if you want to find and tape a programme which is broadcast at 5.30 am on Thursday, you have to look at Wednesday's schedules. This is naturally confusing to parents and educators and does not show much commitment to facilitating either group.

It is interesting to note that the decision to drop much of the educational programming was made at the same time as the change in style of the weather forecasters. One caused outcry, the other nothing. When asked why the change in educational programming had happened, I was told that confidential research carried out in schools on behalf of RTE showed that the schools wanted it that way. This contradicted informal research carried out among teachers which showed that roughly a third of teachers taped the programmes, a third watched them live and a third watched them live and taped them at the same time. So two thirds were watching them live in school.

The emphasis on what schools want also shows that RTE has not grasped the importance of educational television at home. I would go so far as to say that educational television is vital, because it establishes viewing habits. Programming which is primarily entertainment establishes a 'laze and gaze' mindset, which teachers are up against when they use programmes in school. *The Den* also frequently admonishes its viewers to 'Keep your telly right here. Don't touch your telly', when all research shows that the optimum use of television is in very short periods per day.

I understand the financial and commercial constraints under which RTE operates. In many ways it does a very good job. Neither it, nor the State, however, seem to have much concern for the effect of television on children. Some of RTE's home-produced programming, such as the *Morbegs*, is very good and represents a major commitment financially. Likewise, *Draw with Don* and *Animate with Tina* represent programming that stimulates children to do something other than 'space out'. Even *The Den* with its sizeable team is an expensive item to maintain.

RTE would probably claim that all of this will be rectified with the new digital channels. But it is difficult to see how RTE will sustain an entire educational channel when its educational material has been run down so drastically. It would be nice to see more evidence that RTE has a grasp of what this kind of programming would demand. For example, in its *Open Learning* slot, the Canadian *Magic Library* programme was broadcast. It is a great programme, which is open-ended in that the children have to go back to the original book or books mentioned to complete tasks set by the programme. The support material, however, was not available in Ireland, which meant that the most valuable aspect of the programme was nullified. This happened because educational television was so poorly resourced.

There has been deafening silence on the part of the Government, which seems to have no understanding of the central place of television in children's lives. Increases in the licence fee would seem entirely appropriate if conditions were attached such as a requirement to transmit a specific amount of indigenous broadcasting, particularly in the area of children's television. No one seems to have thought much about this, nor seen the importance of it.

Personally, I would support a ban on advertising to children, but I am fully aware that this will not be a panacea. Even if advertising were banned, it is now a fact that some animated programmes are little more than programme-long advertisements for products.

The most notorious example of this is Pokémon. I first became aware of this when my eleven-year-old nephew introduced my six-year-old son to the cartoon. The concept originated in Japan. Pokémon means 'pocket monster'. There were over 150 Pokémon, and the slogan was 'Gotta catch them all'. Then another 101 Pokémon were released in Japan, bringing to 251 the number of Pokémon for children to collect, either as cards or as toys.

The plot concerns Ash, a ten-year-old boy who sets off on his Pokémon journey in order to become a Pokémon master. A Pokémon can be captured and trained and then the trainer takes part in competitions in order to reach the Pokémon league. The cartoons, even though they centre on a form of battling, are not particularly violent. No Pokémon dies. They faint instead and have to be taken to Pokémon recovery centres. The cartoons are not particularly objectionable. What I do object to is the way the whole campaign has been structured to extract every last cent out of parents. They also encourage acquisitiveness and pestering of parents. There are even stories of American children stabbing each other in order to acquire rare Pokémon cards, but we have not reached that stage here!

The following is a short list of the merchandising associated with Pokémon: game cards, trading cards, books, Game Boys and other computer games, Pokédex, toys, balls, films, CDs, figures, wind-up toys, talking toys, soft toys, a tie-in with Burger King, clothes, hats. It is by no means an exhaustive list. They are a craze and each element is tied into the next, so that kids are encouraged to spend more and more time at them. For example, there are certain cards that can only be obtained by going to the Pokémon film. They are quite addictive. I cannot understand their charm but my husband, who is a scientist by training, says the classification of the creatures, all of whom belong to various categories and who 'evolve' in very particular ways, teaches habits of concentration and learning of quite complex material. Be that as it may, Pokémon are a very good example of where television is just an entry point into a whole universe of selling. *Toy.zone.uk* on Sky One, an internet marketing site for toys, promotes the programme. So basically the programme is an extended advertisement for this internet toy shop.

The internet is a tremendous way of parting kids from their money. It is beyond the scope of this chapter to deal with the dangers of the internet, but everyone has a horror story of an innocent search throwing up very strange material. For example, a child who enters 'toys' into a search engine will almost certainly be given results which contain websites for adult sex toys. The Centre for Media Education in Washington ran a campaign to alert parents to the amount of alcohol and tobacco advertising to be found on the web.

For parents, there is hope. It all hinges around responsible parenting. Of course this takes time, which is the one thing parents do not have. But here are a few guidelines.

Watch the programmes with the children and discuss the content

It is important to watch with children. This means that any fears or worries which they have can be dealt with straight away. Research also shows that the parental voice is an important corrective to anything undesirable which is being viewed. If there is an adult present to set a context for what is being viewed, this is of greater influence than the message of the programme itself. A great help in this is to tape programmes for younger children.

Set limits to viewing

This is very important: children need to know that they cannot just slump in front of the television when bored.

Teach about advertisements

From an early age, children can be taught that the primary aim of advertising is to sell products. You can still enjoy witty or well-produced advertisements, while pointing out every time how exaggerated or unreal claims are made for products. This can become a family game.

Tape programmes and create ad-free tapes

Investing in a video recorder is well worthwhile. It means that children are watching television when the parent wishes it, and not according to the schedules of television channels. Cutting out the advertisements is quite simple as you record, and it limits the exposure of children to toy advertisements in particular.

Ensure that babysitters and childminders enforce the same regime

In an age where more and more children are minded during the day, it is important that the other adults who care for them have similar standards.

Establish a family video library

Buying commercial tapes and building up a library of home-recorded programmes means there is always something suitable to watch on a rainy day. With younger children, just as they love the repetition of stories, films and programmes can become family favourites as well.

Encourage hobbies and reading

This is a vital step. Children need alternatives to television and computer games. They also need fresh air. If these habits are established early, they are much easier to sustain.

These and other relatively simple methods can ensure that our children are not brainwashed into mindless consumerism.

Abuse, advertisement and the social purposes of broadcasting

ADRIAN MOYNES

Nowadays it's common to read books and articles arguing that the electronic media do much more than shape the way we perceive the world about us. In fact, they claim that the deep influences of the media are changing our habits of mind. The contention is that television, interactive video games and the like require us to develop processes of instant reaction and to give up our slower, more reflective and considered responses to experience. In the rich and self-styled advanced countries, so the argument goes, youngsters grow up with inhibited imaginations, little appetite for reading and a curtailed ability to entertain themselves. The conclusion of the trend will be to deny children their right to childhood. In short, the verdict is that new media diminish our critical and questioning skills by prizing the image more than the word and by promoting the sensational, the immediate and the superficial. Neil Postman is one of the most articulate and renowned spokespersons for such views with his essays about what he calls, 'the triumphs of one-eyed technology and, in particular, how these triumphs have laid waste some of our most creative, not to mention charming, habits of thought'.

What I will try to do here is to offer some comments and raise some questions within this general area of concern. I am interested in how we think and speak about the electronic media; in our unease about how they may be affecting us; in our suspicions of subliminal influence, manipulation and hidden agendas. I am also fascinated by some of the assumptions we make about the alleged power of the media to transform how we think and feel and relate to others. And finally, I am sceptical about the golden age, the supposed time before the electronic media impoverished our culture and debased it in vulgar commercialism. In preparing these remarks, I was responding to an invitation to be reflective and to offer an overview. For that reason, I have tried to clear a space in which to think about broad trends and tendencies, and so I must declare here at the outset that I have little to say—at least directly—about the immediate and particular circumstances of broadcasting in Ireland now.

Let's begin with an arresting, early perception about the impact of electromagnetic mass communication.

On 14 September 1889, Anton Chekhov wrote a letter to a poet by the name of Pleshcheyev and announced that he'd just completed what many now regard as his first masterpiece, a short fiction entitled *A Boring Story*. He was sending it off to be published in a journal called the *Northern Herald* and looking forward to the debate that would follow the appearance of the story in print. As he put it, 'I further flatter myself with the hope that my rubbish will provoke a certain noisy reaction in the enemy camp, for in our age of telegraphs and telephones, abuse is the sister of advertisement'. This remark captured my attention when I first came across it just about a century after it was written. What attracted me immediately was its epigrammatic balance, its confident alliteration (that's to the translator's credit, of course) and its suggestion of a back-handed compliment to technology—or is it a side-swipe? I also sensed that the line might come in useful one day as a provocative title for some article or other.

Over the last decade, I have often recalled this quotation and found myself speculating about why Chekhov framed his thought in just these words. He had trained as a doctor although ill-health was to cut short his practice. His medical studies at Moscow University gave him a scientific background, and the sufferings of this compassionate, generous man, not to mention the poverty and disease he struggled with in his native country, would of themselves have been enough to persuade him that modern science and technology promised to better the human condition. So, when he said that in an age of telegraphs and telephones, abuse is the sister of advertisement, I'm confident that this was no Luddite onslaught, and certainly no ignorant attack on technological progress.

When you think about Chekhov's stories and plays, the remark is intriguing for other reasons. His creative work is peopled by characters whose lives are constrained, frustrated, even paralysed. They live in a fading world, a society on the slow slide to dissolution. The torpor of their existence, the futility of their interactions, their vain ambitions and their hopelessness—these are noted sensitively and movingly, but Chekhov also probes and dissects their condition by the cold exercise of subtle, moral discriminations. They may live in an age of telegraphs and telephones, but Chekhov's men and women cannot communicate across the width of a dining room, and that is often their deepest tragedy.

At a basic level, of course, Chekhov is saying something that every creative artist knows: if you stick your head above the parapet, you can expect that someone will take a shot at you. For his own part, he clearly relished the prospect of rough-and-tumble debate about his story: a reaction to what he wrote, even a hostile one, would be a sign of life, and Chekhov wanted to make an impact by stirring up a vigorous exchange of views. Yet more than this is implied. In expressing his thought and his emotion in the actual words he chose, Chekhov drew on a perceptive intuition about the new communications media of his time. Clearly, he sensed that through their immediacy and their outreach to masses of people at the same moment, the electromagnetic media are inevitably associated with clamour and contention, with commerce and competition, with hype and with what we now call 'knocking copy'. And if all these things are vulgar, well, they are also vital.

As I say, this is striking as an early formulation of what we may call a social reality of media, by which I mean—how the media affect our everyday experience of the world about us. After more than a century of mass communications, there is by now a well-developed critique of what it means to live with electronic media. For instance, in an essay entitled *Into the Electronic Millennium*, the American Sven Birkerts expresses the opinion that because we take television for granted, we can no longer imagine what it would mean to live without it:

> We cannot see the role that television (or, for our purposes, all electronic communications) has assumed in our lives because there is no independent ledge where we might secure our footing. The medium has absorbed and eradicated the idea of a pre-television past; in place of what used to be we get an ever new and ever-renewable present. The only way we can hope to understand what is happening, or what has already happened, is by way of a severe and unnatural dissociation of sensibility.

Since literature offers us records of human experience from the pre-television era, Birkerts proposes a thought-experiment using the novel as a means of measuring how much the world—and how we experience it—have altered.

> To get a sense of the enormity of the change, you must force yourself to imagine—deeply and in nontelevisual terms—what the world was like a hundred, even fifty, years ago. If the feat is too difficult, spend some time with a novel from the period. Read between the lines and re-construct. Move through the sequence of a character's day and then juxtapose the images and sensations you find with those in the life of the average urban or suburban dweller today.

This is an experiment that we will carry out very shortly. I promise you, it is remarkably instructive and surprising. In setting up the experiment, it will be helpful to recall what at first sight seems to be a well-founded caution against the claims made by advertising.

'Promise, large promise, is the soul of an advertisement', wrote Samuel Johnson in the eighteenth century. With the coming of mass communication, the promises were amplified to such a volume that reason was in danger of being drowned out. Or so G. K. Chesterton claimed in identifying susceptibility to large promise as a characteristic weakness of twentieth-century people.

If you had said to a man in the Stone Age, 'Ugg says Ugg makes the best stone hatchets', he would have perceived a lack of detachment and disinterestedness about the testimonial. If you had said to a medieval peasant, 'Robert the Bowyer proclaims with three blasts of a horn that he makes good bows,' the peasant would have said, 'Well, of course he does,' and thought about something more important. It is only among people whose minds have been weakened by a sort of mesmerism that so transparent a trick as that of advertisement could ever have been tried at all.

What do you think of this? Is it common sense? Or snooty old rubbish? Is it a witty insight? Or does it smack of the po-faced headmaster's address to the upper school? I cite it as an example of the view that no serious-minded person could permit himself or herself to be influenced or taken in by advertising. That if you have a brain in your head, you must be above this sort of thing. That there is a proper interval between abuse and advertisement on the one hand and serious culture on the other. And that it is the hallmark of sane persons to reject stupifying vulgarity—what Chesterton called mesmerism—preferring instead to be conscious and common sensical.

With James Joyce, we may beg to suggest that the matter is more complicated:

> Shite and onions! Do you think I'll print
> The name of the Wellington Monument,
> Sydney Parade and Sandymount tram,
> Downes's cakeshop and Williams's jam?
> I'm damned if I do—I'm damned to blazes!
> Talk about *Irish Names and Places*!
> It's a wonder to me, upon my soul,
> He forgot to mention Curly's Hole.

The satire of Joyce's *Gas from a Burner* is fuelled by anger at a stuffy and respectable refusal to acknowledge how the conscious mind actually works, how it registers the world around it restlessly and randomly, from second to second. This insight became the style and the signature of *Ulysses*. And so to our thought experiment. Remember what Birkerts suggested we do to re-capture the pre-televisual past—'Move through the sequence of a character's day and then juxtapose the images and sensations you find with those in the life of the average urban or suburban dweller today.' Let's do just that. The novel is *Ulysses*, the year is 1904, and Leopold Bloom, canvasser of small advertisements, walks around a Dublin whose reality is present in the trivia and ephemera of modern commercialism:

> In Westland Row he halted before the window of the Belfast and Oriental Tea Company and read the legends of leadpapered packets: choice blend, finest quality, family tea ...

And some minutes later in that same walk, advertising copy prompts speculation about the motive for Ophelia's suicide:

> Mr. Bloom stood at the corner, his eyes wandering over the multicoloured hoardings. Cantrell and Cochrane's Ginger Ale (Aromatic). Clery's summer sale. [...] Hello. *Leah* tonight: Mrs. Bandman Palmer. Like to see her in that again. *Hamlet* she played last night. Male impersonator. Perhaps he was a woman. Why Ophelia committed suicide?

Bloom's head is full of music hall songs, Italian arias and snatches of commercial doggerel such as the incomparable and recurring ad from the *Freeman's Journal*:

> What is home without
> Plumtree's Potted Meat?
> Incomplete.
> With it an abode of bliss.

Undoubtedly one reason why this bit of promotional jingle is lodged in Bloom's mind is that his own domestic circumstances are anything but blissful. In context, then, this ephemeral, silly advertising copy provides a sad, ironic and rich counterpoint to the private life of the character. If he were walking the streets of Dublin today, Bloom might take one hundred steps to better banking or look at a parked car and convince himself to 'Own one and you'll understand, so you will.'

In 1922, James Joyce created the shock of the new by highlighting the fact that modern consciousness internalises these snatches from headlines and hoardings, from the backs of buses and the inanities of print advertising. Trivial flotsam from the external world is channelled into the inner babble that is the normal waking state of mind. It becomes voice-over to the images from without that fill the head, changing from second to second, cutting together faster than the frames in a rock video. Even today, Joyce's enlargement of expression has a power to stop us in our tracks, and not so much because it anticipates the modes of cinema and television, but rather because it follows the movement of mind, attesting a truth about human nature. Joyce is no isolated, 20th century example: the first volume of Laurence Sterne's *Life and Opinions of Tristram Shandy* appeared in 1759, and Charles Dickens often puts onto paper states of consciousnesses that we might delude ourselves by calling characteristically modern.

Apologies for this Cook's Tour of modernism in literature. We'll take a break from it for a while, but I will return to the writers later, for they are prophets of a kind, reading the signs of the times before everyone else. What they tell about life in the age of mass communications includes the difficult truth that there is no fixed gulf between high art and the hard sell, between culture and commercialism. On the contrary, it is the interpenetration, the pell-mell and downright confusion of these and other myriad influences that form our consciousness. A reading of pre-televisual literature will also suggest that we should be wary of any claim that the coming of electronic mass communications has brought with it a step change or paradigm shift in how humans perceive the world, or in how our minds work. I am not convinced by the case as made by writers such as Birkerts when he concludes:

> ... a communications net, a soft and pliable mesh woven from invisible threads, has fallen over everything. The so-called natural world, the place we used to live, which served us so long as the yardstick of all measurements, can now only be perceived through a scrim. Nature was then; this is now. Trees and rocks have receded ...

I don't believe our experience is fractured in this way or that the natural world has retreated from us. To be blunt, I don't know what point is being made here.

I have been talking about media and mind, and taking a backward look over the century past. It's time to look to the future, to speculate, and to ask a few questions about media and money. An article in *The Independent* (21 January 2000) under the headline 'Internet will turn UK high streets into leisure centres' had these opening paragraphs:

> In 20 years the high street will be a place to shop for luxuries and inessentials. Cinemas and coffee shops will help to create an environment in which shopping is seen as a recreation, says a report by an independent research foundation.
>
> Shopping for mundane items such as milk, bread and groceries will be done on the Internet and delivered to homes or collected from a local distribution depot.
>
> ... purchase of goods and services online will become commonplace. Home delivery will be the norm. This reduces the need to travel to work and shop, except for very local shopping for emergency or convenience items.
>
> The trend towards teleworking means people increasingly will leave their homes only for short trips rather than drive to large out-of-town

centres, so neighbourhood shopping facilities will be improved.

The time saved will be used for leisure, and the high street and shopping centres will have to provide more leisure facilities to encourage customers to spend money. 'There is more likely to be a continued emphasis on the combination of leisure and retailing,' says the report ... 'And "boring" shopping will be got out of the way as rapidly and painlessly as possible.'

Articles like this appear frequently, with their motifs of shopping-as-entertainment and the Internet-as-agent-of-social-change. Only time will tell if the predictions are accurate, but the recurring themes of this kind of futurology are few in number and they tend to centre around the notion of entertainment as a personalised and transacted experience, or—to speak English—they beat the drum that shopping must be fun. They also keep step with the notion that to be a citizen is to be a consumer, and with its corollary that the protection of the consumer's interest is pretty much co-incidental with respect for the rights of the citizen. I don't wish to exaggerate on the basis of one newspaper article, but pieces like this set you thinking about how we conceive our society: is it an aggregate of consumers in an economy or a community of citizens?

In the United States, themes like these tend to be dramatised first and most spectacularly. In fact I came across predictions exactly like those reported in *The Independent* when a book entitled *The Entertainment Economy* was published on this side of the Atlantic in 1999. Its sub-title is 'the mega-media forces that are shaping our lives' and its author is Michael J. Wolf, a highly successful media and entertainment consultant. According to his own publicity (his own advertisement), Michael Wolf's 'job is to guide the CEOs of the world's foremost media companies into the future of a business that never stops changing and expanding internationally'. Bearing in mind Dr Johnson's warning about 'promise, large promise', I will quote from the fly-leaf of the book to give a flavour of what awaits the reader of *The Entertainment Economy*.

Every so often an author explains our culture in such a new and original way that from that day on we see the world around us in a new light. From *Understanding the Media* by Marshall McLuhan to Nicholas Negroponte's *Being Digital*, the books that have shown us the clearest vision of the future have been those that recognize the central role of mass media.

In *The Entertainment Economy*, Michael J. Wolf, the industry's most in-demand strategist, demonstrates that media and entertainment have moved beyond culture to become the driving force of the global economy. From London to Lagos, from Singapore to Seattle, from New York to New Delhi, every business is locked in the same battle for consumer attention that film producers and television programmers deal with on a daily basis. Consumer businesses, just like entertainment businesses, have to turn to content for the competitive edge. As adviser to companies and individuals such as Disney, Rupert Murdoch, Bertelsmann and Intel, Wolf is known by industry insiders as the moguls' secret weapon.

In a sentence, Wolf's thesis is that 'Locally, globally, internationally, we are living in an entertainment economy' where the successful companies know that their future growth depends upon their ability to add the e-factor to their products and services. The e-factor is entertainment, and Wolf argues that whether you're selling financial services or finger food, you must convince the customer that doing business with you will be more fun than shopping from your competitors.

This book is very American, culturally and stylistically; and it embodies an extraordinary contradiction for it is the product of a mind that is at once sophisticated, worldly-wise, and yet naively unselfconscious. It is, as they say, upfront and in your face. For example, at one point Wolf is illustrating his belief that 'once you start entertaining, it had better be the best there is'. He tells the story of his company's annual three-day cruise to the Bahamas which he describes as 'a fun way to say thank you to the business school interns who spend their summers with us'. The anecdote continues:

Last year we booked three days on Royal Caribbean's flagship, *Sovereign of the Seas*. We pulled out of Miami on a Friday evening. The shirts and ties of our Park Avenue headquarters were exchanged for golf shirts and baggy surfer shorts. The business-day libations of Perrier and cappuccino were replaced by pina coladas, coco locos, and Bahama mamas. We had a good time. We bonded. We were into the beginning of a three-day megaparty.

The next morning, shortly after awakening as our ship gently slid into its mooring in Nassau, my family and I were all in dreamland when a low, resonant steamship horn tooted the opening bars of the *Pinocchio* theme: *When you wish upon a staaaar* ... My son, Morgan, stood on tiptoe to look out the porthole and let go with a 'Wow!' As high as my opinion is of my young heir, I know how relatively easy it is to impress a preschooler, so I sat up and joined him at the porthole. 'Wow!' I echoed. There stretched out before us was the *Disney Magic*, the $350 million cruise ship on its maiden voyage. Standing out in bold relief against the blue Caribbean sky, one could see its water slide (as my son can tell you, our ship didn't have one), its ESPN Skybox lounge (our ship didn't have one), and its Mickey Mouse-shaped swimming pool (it would have been a trademark infringement if our ship had had one)...

... for the next sixteen hours that we were in port, all the talk on our ship was how we all wanted to be on that other ship. I would have expected this from Morgan, but when a twenty-six year old genius from Harvard Business School says, 'Michael, can you believe that ship?', I knew that though we were just trying to show our troops a good time, in the world of entertainment, if you don't have what seems like the latest and coolest thing, then you have a bad case of loseritis.

This story raises many questions, not least of them—'Why didn't he drop the Harvard brat into the sea?' We should not be deceived by the folksy style of our good ole upbeat buddy in the boardroom—this is actually a work of some substance and insight—I say 'some'. From the commercial perspective, it's refreshingly honest about the economic forces energising the media, mass entertainment and mass communications. Here is a book about how the big bucks are made.

I have taken time and space to quote from *The Entertainment Economy* because its language, its tone and its style are good illustrations of a climate of discussion, of how the market thinks and talks about broadcasting and mass media today. Works like this are influential and in many quarters they set the limits for debate about powerful cultural forms such as television and the Internet. That's not surprising for it accords with the mood of the moment. People today are impatient with regulation and state intervention, with intrusive government and the nanny state. The free play of market forces is advocated as the engine of prosperity, and we are told, for example, that the last thing we need in these circumstances is old-fashioned, unimaginative, torpid state broadcasting. Nowadays, the market will meet our needs, giving us choice and quality, what we want, when we want it.

The reality, of course, is that a discussion limited to market considerations offers a narrow perspective on broadcasting, new media, and their social purposes. I don't like the tone of *The Entertainment Economy* but I have few, if any, substantive points of disagreement with it. You don't need to be a Harvard MBA to assent to a number of Michael Wolf's central tenets and contentions. For example, I accept that broadcasting is radically commercial; that concentrations of media ownership are carving out enlarged spheres of influence; that the Internet is not about to obliterate broadcasting; and finally, that the media changes we are now experiencing are evolutionary rather than revolutionary. However, it seems to me that this discussion gets really interesting only when you start to deal with the things that the book leaves unsaid.

Let me try to develop this point. In accepting that broadcasting is radically commercial, I refer to the inescapable power of commercial considerations in the spread of television and radio. An item of elementary knowledge in the media studies class is the fact that radio programmes of variety, sport, news and information were first devised as selling propositions, or killer applications, to boost consumer interest in wireless receivers when they were launched on the American market early in the last century. A generation later, US network television built its power base on its ability to aggregate vast audiences of consumers to whom commercial messages—advertisements—were directed. The underlying dynamic of these media was market growth. Television and radio were, and are, and will be for the masses—that is how they make money in the market. And when you talk about the economics of mass media, it is misleading to speak of niche appeal or minority interest. This is so because the only profitable niche is a big one. Or more accurately, there are only two kinds of profitable minority. The first is a huge minority in a giant market, and the second is a tiny minority of very rich people paying a hefty premium for exclusive service.

It's necessary and healthy to acknowledge these facts of life. To do so is not to sell the pass of public service broadcasting. By recognising the commercial reality, we merely begin the discussion—we certainly do not exhaust it. This is another way of saying that broadcasting need not be confined by the commercialism of its origins and its environment. On the contrary, it is possible to intervene in the market, to set purposes and objectives for broadcasting other than simply commercial ones. And it is even possible to employ commercial means to secure those objectives. This is what public broadcasting in Europe has done historically and what it continues to do as we step into the next phase in the evolution of broadcasting. This pursuit of social purposes in broadcasting may be unfashionable in some quarters and it certainly goes against the grain of economic liberalism, yet it continues to be central and necessary to the democratic order.

An editorial (15 January 2000) on the merger of AOL and Time/Warner in *The Economist* magazine (or newspaper, as it calls itself) encapsulated this tension between market reality and social purpose in broadcasting. The leader writer predicts that the future of broadcasting is narrowcasting, that is, the supply of niche programming that appeals to what makes people different, as opposed to what they have in common. The market will offer special interest television channels to cater for a spectrum of appetites in the manner of the magazines on display in Eason's. Subscribers will cluster around the menu of channels that interest them, and television will lose its convocational role, its focus for mass attention in society. In *The Economist'* view this will be no loss because 'broadcasting has always appealed to the lowest common denominator'. In support of this rash generalization, the leader cites 'new-media prophet' George Gilder, quoting an observation of his which is only half as smart as it sounds: 'Television is not vulgar because people are vulgar—it is vulgar because people are similar in their prurient interests and sharply different in their civilised concerns.'

Leaving aside the consideration that democracy is a vulgar commodity, this assertion is questionable on at least two grounds. First, because prurience takes many forms and people's low tastes are actually highly diversified (if you want proof, look at Channel 4's *So Graham Norton*). I confess that I am very choosy in my prurience and I'm sure that you are every bit as discriminating: hence the expression which recognises an important truth of human nature, 'whatever turns you on'. Secondly and with all due respect to *The Economist* and Mr Gilder, sex, shopping and violence are not all that we have in common, for we can and do make common cause about civilised concerns such as freedom of speech, diversity of expression and representative democracy. This brings me to the case of Norman Horowitz.

Norman Horowitz is an independent producer in the United States, a man with long experience of the television industry and now a Governor of the Banff Television Festival. Here is someone who is clear-headed about the market realities of broadcasting and sharply aware of the abuse to which those realities are prone. In one of his recent comments on the state of US broadcasting he made this point: 'I have noticed during my career in television that included service at CBS, Viacom, Columbia Pictures, Polygram and MGM that the greater the power of these organizations, the greater their predisposition to abuse.' By abuse, Horowitz refers specifically to concentrations of media power. He recalls that 'From the beginning of television in this country, three unelected Americans, Bill Paley, David Sarnoff and Leonard Goldenson, decided what America watched on television.'

Horowitz calls these three men 'the media moguls of the mid 20th Century'. As we enter the twenty-first century, a series of global media mergers is reshaping television and in the United States, Horowitz now argues that four men are emerging 'who will control the vast majority of what we see in all forms of television, what we learn about our world, what news we hear, what documentaries are made, and most importantly, have purview over our electoral process, by exposing or not exposing candidates to the electorate in a manner never envisioned by the FCC, Justice Department, or in fact by the framers of our Constitution.'

The four men are Rupert Murdoch, Micheal Eisner, Sumner Redstone and Gerald Levin. Horowitz poses the same question about each man, and one instance will suffice for my purpose here:

> Is it a good idea for Gerald Levin to control ABC-TV and ABC Radio, 10 TV and 30 radio stations, ESPN, Disney Channel, A&E, E!, Lifetime, Miramax, Walt Disney Pictures, Touchstone, Hollywood, Hyperion, ESPN Magazine, Walt Disney Records, Mammoth, Lyric Street,

Parks in Florida, California, France and Japan, Anaheim Angels, Mighty Ducks, Disney Stores, Go Network Internet Portal, and much more?

As it happens, a few days after these words were written, Gerald Levin was swallowed by AOL—TV, radio, print, portals, theme parks and all. Which underlines the point.

Horowitz concludes, 'Our nation could speak with many voices, but we don't. It's scary, isn't it?'

Who knows how many years of apogee, decline and fall are in store for these media empires. Perhaps they will fracture and tumble as quickly as they formed. As of now, they are the best argument for vigilant and effective regulation in the public interest. Anything that powerful has to be worth watching, in every sense of the verb.

The social purposes of broadcasting arise from the democratic life of the community. Reliable, impartial news and information, free debate, diverse cultural self-expression, minority language rights, a sense of being connected to the life of the people watching and listening—all these values are central and not marginal to our quality of life. Securing them is a challenge that must be met every day. It is not good enough to say that the market will serve these ends across a spectrum of narrowcasting. And it's certainly not acceptable to argue that if the market fails to provide them, well then, it's because there is no demand for them, which in turn must mean that people place no value on them.

It is not easy to argue this case today, to direct attention to the essential social purposes of broadcasting. Part of the difficulty stems from the inescapable commercial ambience of broadcasting and its unceasing competitive struggle. Another part of the problem is rooted in that high-minded contempt which confuses popular culture with the lowest common denominator. Out of that confusion arises a crisis of belief in broadcasting's ability to serve any purpose other than practising mesmerism in order to take money from the gullible. And in part, it's due to the fact that we broadcasters can fail in our core undertaking, and sometimes fail spectacularly. But the effort of communicating with ourselves is not only worthwhile, it is—as Chekhov perceived—essential, even if it means that we must keep company with the vulgar sisters, abuse and advertisement.

Are you being served? Commercial versus public broadcasting

URSULA HALLIGAN

The title 'Are you being served? Commercial versus public broadcasting' assumes that commercial and public service television are different beasts, holding totally opposed positions. While in theory they should indeed be very different, the actual distinction in reality is rapidly dissolving. Enormous changes in technology, society and the marketplace have revolutionized the world of television and blurred traditional differences between the two. These days, whether it's public service or commercial television, it's the viewer that's calling the shots.

Most people know that the technologies behind the telephone, television and computer are converging. But not everyone is aware of the convergence taking place between commercial and public service broadcasting to a point where soon they will be little or no difference. If things go on as they are, the traditional role of public broadcasting will soon be obsolete.

RTE, BBC and other old-style public broadcasters across Europe are rapidly re-inventing themselves in the face of major structural changes taking place in the industry. The end result is not public service broadcasting—as we've known it—but a new creature altogether—a confused hybrid—trying to straddle both the commercial and public service worlds, and failing.

Thirty years ago, most European countries had just one national television station. In Ireland, that station was RTE. Unlike newspapers—that operated under normal market conditions—Governments sought to regulate television and supervise its content. They did this for two reasons: broadcast wavelengths were scarce and considered to be public property *and* politicians believed that television was an extremely powerful force with huge potential to inform *and* influence public opinion.

Just read any of the Dáil or Senate debates in 1960 on the Broadcasting Authority Bill that set up RTE and you'll sense the fascination and wonder television evoked. Michael Hilliard, the Minister for Posts and Telegraphs at the time, told the Senate that television had become 'a household god' in other countries 'with more power ... than was ever held by the ancient idols. If this is so elsewhere today', he said, what might the power of television be 'here in ten or fifteen years time when there may be a television set in every home'.

When setting up the new station, the Government opted for the British public broadcasting model, but one funded by a mixed revenue stream of advertising and licence fee. Irish politicians wanted Telefís Éireann to showcase the
national culture and provide opportunities for the development of the Irish language, the arts, drama, education and entertainment. On items of controversy
or public debate, the station was to ensure impartial and objective coverage.
For some, it also had another duty, that of guarding the national image. Former
taoiseach Seán Lemass gave the new broadcasting authority the following
advice when it first met in 1960:

> Because the image of themselves which is offered by a national televi-
> sion service can influence the people of any nation to aspire to a better
> life, the pretext of objectivity should not be allowed to excuse the
> undue representation of our faults. What you should aim to present is a
> picture of Ireland and the Irish as we would like to have it, although
> our hopes and aims may well be helped by the objective presentation of
> facts in association with constructive comment.

Or, in other words: 'Show as we'd like to be seen, but occasionally tell us the
truth.'

It wasn't a million miles away from what the first BBC director general, Lord
John Reith, was saying some years earlier. For him, too, public service broadcasting, was 'the voice of the nation'. It had a duty to 'educate, inform and
entertain' and in that order of priority. Reith believed broadcasting should lead
public taste rather than pander to it. In 1925 he wrote: 'He who prides himself
on giving what he thinks the public wants is often creating a fictitious demand
for lower standards which he himself will then satisfy.' For Reith, as for
Lemass, people needed to be told what was good for them.

It was that philosophy which infused the early public service broadcasters. It's
odd but there has never been a formal, 'definitive definition' of public service
broadcasting, much to the frustration of commercial rivals who get tetchy over
perceived incursions into their patch, yet can't cry foul because there is no rule-
book. Instead, over the years a loose set of principles, epitomizing the essence
of public service broadcasting, has evolved. These include the ability to:

• Reach everyone. Like the postal system or any other state service,
  television was to serve the entire nation, including remote areas. Viewers
  were regarded more as citizens than consumers.
• Fortify democracy by informing and educating citizens and by providing
  programmes for minorities.
• Promote national identity and social stability by embodying national
  values.

- Be independent from vested interests, including the Government of the day.
- Make programmes that appealed to a wide range of tastes.
- Be funded either entirely or via some element of public finance.
- Be accountable to the public and not to market forces.

That was the way the world of public service broadcasting looked years ago. Now, each of the characteristics listed above is under assault in some form or other. Public service broadcasters no longer hog national populations all to themselves. Technological, social and economic changes have chipped away at the foundations that gave rise to public broadcasters. Economies and governments have moved in favour of the marketplace.

Moreover, competition has entered the scene and carved up the great monolithic, national audience. In this new world order, there are no national frontiers. Satellites beam down on a borderless world. Every European country has more than one national broadcaster and can receive several foreign channels via cable and satellite.

Public service broadcasters face a dilemma. If they fight to retain their viewers, they have to enter the ratings war with commercial stations. But doing that means churning out more light entertainment and diluting their public service remit to educate, inform and cater for minority interests.

If they don't compete, many believe they face relegation to niche status or banishment to the periphery like the weak public broadcasters in the United States and Australia. They think going this route means losing the mass audience and that would make it difficult to justify a licence fee. Others would argue that this needn't be the case, that far from becoming a ghetto on the fringes, they would become an oasis, an oasis of the very best in public service broadcasting, making programmes that the commercial market fails to provide.

Three key changes explain how the television industry has arrived at this point. The first concerns the way society has changed: the age of the individual is upon us. Political parties, churches, trade unions and other groupings no longer carry the considerable clout they once had. Traditional values and allegiances are breaking down. People are more discriminating about defining their needs and managing themselves. Lives are more complex; tastes more diverse; expectations higher. By such standards, Lord Reith's view of public service broadcasting appears paternalistic and elitist. Even a BBC policy statement in 1995 conceded as much when it said:

> They (i.e. the audience) are more discerning, more aware of their power and their rights as consumers of broadcasting, less willing to be patronized or talked down to, less ready to accept someone else's definition of what they should enjoy.

The magic of what's happening at the moment is that there isn't just a new appetite out there among viewers; there are also new technologies to feed it. Instead of being force-fed carrots and fruit and all things good by public broadcasters, other menus are now on the table. That brings me to the second key change that has brought us to this point: technology. Television has changed both in the way we receive it *and* in the way it makes a profit. Years ago, it was delivered using the 'terrestrial' network of analogue signals. This system had limited capacity, generated a handful of channels and was government-regulated. These restrictions created a market dynamic. The reason television made money was because there were so few channels to start with and because it reached a mass audience for advertisers and helped create powerful brand names.

The profit dynamic changed when technology threw up two more delivery systems: cable and satellite. These systems make money by designing channels for special interest groups and generate not only advertising but also subscription income. These include lucrative niche channels like Sky Sports, MTV, Nickelodeon and the Movie Channel. Interestingly, some—including the History Channel—cover more and more niches which were usually considered as public interest programming.

The market dynamic changed again when digital compression came along. It exploded the capacity of all three delivery systems to enable people to receive not just hundreds but thousands of different channels. It also reduced production costs but ignited another totally new market. Suddenly, programmes *and* sporting events, which we had all watched free of charge for years, became precious commodities with exclusive rights. Watching many of them in the future will be on a pay-per-view basis.

The third key change that has taken place involves the 'nation state'. In the past, public service broadcasters prided themselves on promoting a sense of national identity and facilitating shared national experiences. Years ago, we all watched the same programmes at the same time and talked about them the next day. However, the weakening of the nation state as an entity and the spread of new channels—including global media conglomerates like Murdoch's Sky TV—have changed all that. If anything, EU membership, global alliances among media players, the internet and increasing access to foreign sources of news and entertainment have created a new, trans-national culture. Viewers are spoilt for choice these days and straying fast in various directions. The national audience no longer hangs together as a homogeneous lump.

It is an irony in some ways that television—once the great unifier—could become the great divider because of its future potential to tailor schedules to an infinite number of individual preferences. In the United States, the concept of 'Me TV' is currently being developed. This is where television sets are

designed to select programming to suit the viewer's known tastes and preferences. It's like having your very own customized television channel.

From the public service broadcaster's position, the world has become a very
hostile place. The new environment is forcing stations like the BBC and RTE
to face up to difficult questions about their relevance to modern society. Soon,
both will be just two of hundreds and eventually thousands of channels flooding
the airwaves. The fact that they are still around today is a measure of how each
has adapted to the marketplace. The question is: how much further down that
road can they go without abandoning their public service remit completely?

Indeed, some critics would argue that RTE already overly embraces the
commercial to the detriment of its public service brief. Certainly, the station's
drift to commercialism is reflected in its dominant reliance on advertising—
almost two thirds of revenue.

Preserving the public service remit on the one hand, and competing with
commercial stations to retain market share and advertising on the other, is a
difficult circle to square. It's little wonder that every so often the critics let fly
and lambaste the station for everything: from being too commercial to abandoning serious drama and current affairs for soaps, quizzes and chat shows. Part
of the problem is that there is no formal definition of what constitutes public
service broadcasting—no measurable set of objectives to meet.

The incongruous mix of state and market in RTE has also thrown up some
bizarre situations. Even though the station is a semi-state body, it refuses to
reveal details of the earnings of its top presenters. Then, there's the Freedom of
Information Act: what might happen if I, or someone on my behalf, put in a
request to see the notes of a story made by an RTE news journalist?

As Joe Mulholland, RTE's Managing Director—Television, wrote shortly
before he retired: 'For how long more can we play two roles simultaneously: a
commercial operator whose existence depends alarmingly on what it can earn
in the marketplace and that of a public service broadcaster?'

Commercial rivals have been asking the same question for some time! Especially when they find themselves competing in the marketplace with a public
broadcaster funded in part by a licence fee. Several commercial stations, including TV3, are pursuing this issue at EU level. It's not the licence fee *per se* that
they have a problem with: it's the failure of Governments to define precisely
what public service broadcasting is, and to introduce real transparency in the
verification of this process.

RTE doesn't have to be caught in this bind. The world of broadcasting may
be undergoing one of the most radical restructurings in its short history, but
that doesn't mean there isn't life after digital for the station. There are options
to be explored.

The Government, for instance, could cut the umbilical cord with RTE in a
phased way and let it float free as a commercial entity. That would certainly

keep rivals happy because, in one fell swoop, it would solve the licence fee row. It would also raise questions about what would happen to the station's public service obligations.

Another option is for RTE to go down the niche route. This could provide a highly effective re-definition of public service broadcasting and its relevance to Ireland. By going the niche route, the organisation might consciously retreat from competition in the commercial market, and become a national resource for those elements of public discourse and culture which inevitably get squeezed out in that commercial market by their need to effectively 'sell' provable numbers to advertisers. If you've got to prove to advertisers that your drama output attracts and holds mass audiences, then—as sure as night follows day—you go the soap opera route.

If, however, you are funded by the State to provide and preserve drama which is unlikely to attract the mass audience, but is nevertheless worth doing, then you can avoid soaps completely, commissioning new and innovative work and showcasing the great playwrights in technically superb productions.

Similarly, if you are seeking a mass audience for your current affairs output, you will tend to favour the Roger Cook-type documentary. You may even be pushed by your need for numbers into a situation where—as happened on Channel 4—independent producers supplying high-audience documentaries end up faking the more dramatic bits of their programming.

If, on the other hand, you are providing a thoughtful alternative to that type of programming, you could certainly create a platform for detailed discussion of issues which, while they may not result in your presenter being satisfactorily beaten up on screen, will satisfy the intellectual needs of a non-mass audience.

However, there are several problems about RTE going down the niche route. Firstly, it would require a strong, visionary approach, developed and implemented by some agency or body outside of any of the existing broadcasting entities, public service or commercial, and detached, also, from political intervention.

Without such an external agency or authority, this alternative model will never develop. You can't ask organisations like RTE to shrink, to pull out of areas where it regards itself as highly successful and where it has a considerable track record of development.

But even if it were possible to create a radio and television entity along these lines—that is, supplying programming that the mass market doesn't seek—why do we assume that it is a good thing that certain categories—the arts, literature, opera, that may not draw a huge audience—should be looked after by the public broadcaster?

Assume, for example, that the Government decided to set RTE's face towards becoming a national repository of serious music, drama, etc.—all the elements in Reith's old elitist model. You quickly run into questions like: Why

should RTE be the archive for, say, folklore/folkmusic when we now have separate state agencies vested with more or less that responsibility?

Why should people who want to watch, say, the works of Ibsen have that
pleasure supported by the State when people who want to watch the works of
Geri Halliwell, former Spice Girl, have to take advertising as part of the delivery system? Could we possibly be repeating the: 'we know better than the little
people' philosophy of the BBC's Lord Reith?

Why should 'serious material' be in such need of protection when we have,
in this country at this time, twice or three times the number of third-level grad-
uates than we had in the 1930s and 1940s? Have we so little faith in this high-
ly-educated audience that we don't believe they will influence the programming
plans of commercial stations? On this last point, it's worth drawing attention to
a significant aspect of the internet.

It's appropriately called the Gutenberg Project, its name harking back to the
invention of printing. In the centuries directly after the invention of printing,
there was a kind of public service flavour to the spread of the printed word:
books were scarce and precious. They were a valuable part of society's understanding of itself. People could come to where the books were kept and read
them, but you couldn't let them run away with the books themselves, so the
books were chained up—elitist, protective thinking.

Books escaped from that thinking and became the first great communicative
force to change the way people thought and acted. When the paperback
arrived, the book moved decisively from its attributed role of informing and
educating an elite to entertaining the masses long before television did. Pulp
fiction gave the masses huge access to books and a multiplicity of choice. In
theory, serious literature should have been wiped out and, in theory, someone
should have set up a publicly-funded publishing entity to make sure that the
great works from previous centuries didn't die out altogether—a sort of RTE,
but for books.

Instead, a more exciting thing has happened. Literate people all over the
world, in their thousands, became part of this Gutenberg Project. They don't
know each other, but each one has a book—a classic—they love and want to
share. So they sit down and input that book (out of copyright, of course) and it
becomes available, free of charge and downloadable, on the internet. There are
now thousands of books in that library, with hundreds more coming on-stream
every month.

Preservation of elitist material is a very good thing, but it's no longer something which requires state subvention. In the western world, television and
radio are suffering attrition of viewers and listeners because of what's available
on the internet, which is opening up all sorts of possibilities that we never
dreamed of before and giving power back to the people.

The age of the individual has arrived. The technology is there to satisfy an

infinite range of needs and tastes. The keys of the kingdom need no longer be
guarded by public broadcasters. So, in answer to the title of this chapter, 'Are
you being served?—Commercial versus public broadcasting', the answer is:
We're being served somewhat at the moment, but if the powers that be really
want to serve the needs of the nation, they ought to radically reframe the whole
broadcasting scene and re-define public service broadcasting so that it has a real
meaning and function for the twenty-first century.

Economic and financial journalism as a public service

GEORGE LEE

One of the fundamental differences between communicating via the print media and communicating via television news broadcasts relates to the small amount of time available to get one's story across in a broadcast. Typically, at the moment, an RTE television news report lasts between one and a half and two minutes, with the mid-point—one minute and forty-five seconds—being the norm. Typically also, one can expect to use a maximum of three words for every second of broadcast. This means that to get a story across in a television news report one has to do so with the use of just 300 words. Of course, the use of appropriate pictures can help enormously in explaining a story, and some pictures are indeed worth a thousand words. Why else would television news have such a large impact on audiences?

Consider, for instance, the Ethiopian famines, the war in Kosovo or the Gulf war; innocent people, including children, starving in Ethiopia; burnt-out houses and villages and the exodus of refugees from Kosovo; the night skies over Iraq lit up with the incessant bombardment from American and British battleships in the Persian Gulf. It's never too difficult, in such cases, to get the message across about what is happening on a daily basis to a wide audience when the television images speak for themselves.

What is much more difficult to get across in a 300-word television report is any analysis of the famine or the war. Why, for instance, has the famine or war occurred? What are the politics behind it? Who has a vested interest in prolonging it and what is that interest? What are the political implications, locally and internationally? What are its social implications? What are the economic implications? Is Western intervention a good thing or a bad thing? The list goes on and on and can be applied to any event of significance regardless of how well the pictures show the daily events.

The answers to any such questions are never easy. They are usually very complex, requiring considerable analysis, and can rarely be illustrated with stunning pictures. This is where the major challenge comes in for a television reporter. How does one analyse complex issues and explain them to a very varied audience with the use of just 300 words?

One way is to include analysis on an on-going basis, gradually building it up as the story develops. This way the audience gets a deeper and better under-standing of the issues as the story unfolds. Not surprisingly, this is the way tele-vision news covers many big global stories and it is a method that works effectively.

Another way is to use words and a tone that have impact. This is especially important if you cannot rely on pictures that have impact. Every one of the 300 words available to a television news reporter is precious. One has to get to the point quickly. This is especially so if the event to be reported on is not a run-ning story, like a war or a famine, but is a once-off or sudden event or happen-ing that was not anticipated by the public.

Economic and financial analysis and reporting may seem a million miles from a war or a famine. However, the principles of getting the message across are the same. If the pictures tell the story they makes the job easier. If not, then I have to cover things as running stories, constantly updating and adding new pieces of analysis to build up a better public understanding of the issues over time. For me, the work I did with my RTE colleague Charlie Bird to uncover the National Irish Bank offshore tax story falls into this category.

Then, of course, there are the situations in which important economic events happen without any notice. Just like in other areas of reporting, the best way to get the message across about such events is to use language and tone in a man-ner that reflects the seriousness and the meaning of these events. For me, 'Bud-get 2000' and the controversy it sparked definitely falls into this category. That budget was unusual because it included some very significant and unexpected changes in terms of taxation and government spending that went to the heart of the way families are treated by the Irish taxation system.

This chapter deals with my involvement in both of these stories. Perhaps there are lessons to be learned from them about financial reporting as a public service.

The Central Bank
In one of my first jobs after college, I worked as an economist with the Central Bank. It was during my formative years and I thought I would be an economist there for the rest of my life. Needless to say, that turned out to be untrue. I only stayed for two years, but during that time, through work, coffee breaks and socialising events, I learned a lot about the mindset within the Central Bank in relation to its dealings with the media in the late 1980s and early 1990s.

I know for a fact that there were many conversations about newspapers and journalists. In the main, they weren't nice conversations. The prevailing view was that journalists are not very bright, never understand what they are told, will twist things to get a story, and should never be trusted. One motto that was repeated again and again in the presence of younger staff was that, when jour-nalists ask questions about bank matters, don't give any answer and, if you refuse to answer for long enough, they will go away. The thing I now find so amazing is that nine or ten years ago that is exactly what happened. The media did ask the bank questions, the bank frequently didn't answer, and the media did go away.

For instance, the Central Bank used to have press conferences to publicise its Quarterly Bulletin in the later 1980s. But then the Bank stopped these conferences because of some coverage it was unhappy about. Instead, they just resorted to giving out their economic bulletin without any briefing. And when journalists asked questions they never really got anywhere. Everything was secret and couldn't be discussed.

I came into journalism having experienced that kind of background only ten years ago. Now I'm with RTE and things have changed in relation to economic reporting. But most of the changes have been very recent. The Central Bank has got much better at dealing with the media and holds more regular briefings. However, up until last year the bank, a State-owned public institution, would allow me to bring an RTE camera into its press conferences only on condition that we turned off the sound. This was despite the fact that everybody in newspapers could report verbatim what officials of the bank had said at those press conferences.

I made some protestations about this and some top brass at the bank held a meeting to discuss my complaints. They agreed I could be allowed to interview one of the bank executives after the press briefings to have a sound-clip for television but insisted that RTE could not record sound during its briefings. I was told that the fear within the bank was that the camera might capture what some executive said in a moment when he or she was unguarded.

Eventually we told them that RTE was not going to come down to its briefings anymore unless we could turn on the sound on the television camera for the whole briefing. And finally in recent months they caved in. We got our way and RTE, the national broadcaster, was allowed to record the sound of Central Bank economists briefing the press about the bank's economic views. It took until the end of the century for a television station to be given the same reporting access to Central Bank briefings as had been given to newspaper journalists. And it was only in the past year that we finally got a Central Bank economist to do an interview for the camera about non-monetary economic matters.

I know some of the economists at the Central Bank reasonably well. I know for a fact that they are as good at explaining economics to economists as any of their peers in the private sector banks and stockbrokers. But it seems the Central Bank has a huge institutional fear about telling ordinary people what it is about the economy that is important.

This Central Bank experience is just one example of something that is happening throughout all those economic, banking and financial areas of our society. These areas have been opening up in a massive way over a very short period of time. My view is that this 'opening up' is a response to the fact that everybody is beginning to realise that all this information about economics and budgets is for people. It's not just for economists. And it's not just for tax experts. It's about our society and it impacts on our people.

Looking at these types of issues, and considering these types of experiences, it seems clear to me that economic and financial journalism has come a long way. And in doing so, I have no doubt that it is doing an enormous public service. However, dealing with organisations and institutions like the Central Bank is only one element of economic and financial journalism these days. My own experience with the National Irish Bank story and the way that story unfolded reveals a very different side.

National Irish Bank (NIB)

My involvement in this story began on Monday afternoon, 12 January 1998. Charlie Bird received a phone call in the RTE newsroom from a trade union activist who told him he had a story which had the potential to be the poor man's version of the Ansbacher scandal. That Ansbacher scandal revolved around illicit payments into offshore bank accounts, systematic tax evasion, golden circles, and possible political corruption.

The activist explained that a few years back National Irish Bank had linked up with Clerical Medical International (CMI) and established a scheme to help some NIB customers technically to put money offshore. But the money stayed on deposit in the bank in numbered accounts. The customers were given the numbers and easy access to their money but, because technically the money was offshore, the Revenue Commissioners could never pry into it. The bank, the customer and CMI all gained. The State and the ordinary taxpayer were the big losers.

The following day the trade union activist handed us a sheet of paper. It contained eleven scribbled eight-digit numbers, two four-digit numbers with the letters 'PP' before them, one with the prefix 'PA', four amounts ranging from £40,500 to £580,883, a few other scrawls and then a key phrase: '173 accounts altogether'. These account numbers and amounts had been copied down from a computer screen in National Irish Bank over a year earlier. They all referred to CMI portfolio accounts.

One CMI printout for a man from the West of Ireland clearly showed his money was not on deposit in his local branch as had been described by the trade union activist. Instead it showed his £106,000 investment was split between the shares of leading Irish companies and offshore unit trust funds managed by international fund managers including Fidelity, Fleming, Gartmore and CMI.

I examined the hand-scrawled numbers on the photocopied page for almost three days. Some things about it were clear enough. The eight-digit figures down the left-hand side were the numbers for NIB accounts held in CMI's name in trust for NIB customers. The two 'PP' and the one 'PA' numbers were the personal portfolio code numbers associated with these accounts. Obviously the four amounts with the pound signs were the values of the relevant individual portfolios at the date the note was copied from the bank's computer. The sheet suggested that date was 22 November 1996, indicated by 22 over 11 over 96 in the upper right hand corner. It also suggested there was a wide range of investors involved in the scheme. The four amounts listed on the sheet ranged from as little as £40,000 to as much as £600,000. Apart from these four, there were 169 others involved, bringing the total to '173 accounts altogether'.

We were told the investment scheme was set up in the early 1990s. The words 'opened 12/11' beside one account suggested the investment scheme was being marketed as recently as November 1996, the same month this reading was taken from the bank's computer. The implication was that the bank may still have been actively marketing the scheme at that time. The number '95 15 20' at the top of the list remained a mystery, but we would learn later that it was the bank sorting code for the NIB head office branch in Dublin into which all the CMI accounts were moved sometime in 1994.

Revenue Commissioners

Throughout the 1980s, certain Irish banks were flush with accounts which had been deliberately set up to avoid the gaze of the Revenue Commissioners. These included illegal non-resident accounts and accounts in false names. In most cases these accounts had been originally opened with at least the knowledge, and in many cases the assistance, of senior bank branch personnel. But in the early 1990s the tax climate changed. The Revenue Commissioners and the Central Bank wanted the illegal non-resident accounts regularised.

The offshore investment plan hatched in the financial services division of NIB had many attractions: CMI would pay National Irish Bank sizeable commissions for each investor they attracted to the scheme. The funds transferred to CMI could then be rapidly re-deposited back to the NIB branches from which they came, so each branch's deposit base would remain intact. Depositors would surely be happy to have the ultimate cloak of anonymity, a numbered account that the Revenue Commissioners could never access. Arrangements could be put in place to ensure the depositors could access their funds over the counter at their local NIB branch.

Some of the bank's non-resident accounts would be effectively 'cleaned up' as requested by the Central Bank. The CMI personal portfolio was a legitimate insurance-based investment product. Clerical Medical International was a blue chip company with a better credit rating that National Irish Bank itself. It had all the appearance of the ultimate solution. There could be winners all round.

We were told that the situation where a client had a portfolio investment divided between managed funds 'was the exception' and that 'most of the investors had their money lodged back on deposit in their branch and they just came down to the bank and took it out over the counter.'

Sometime in 1994, NIB head office decided this whole CMI scheme was getting too messy. People were taking money out all over the country. A decision was taken to centralise all the CMI accounts in Dublin where they could be better controlled. The vast majority of the investors left their money on deposit, as interest rates in Ireland were very high in the early 1990s.

NIB bank managers described how people were brought into the scheme. All NIB branches were contacted by the bank's Financial Advice and Service Division (FASD). They were looking for customers with big deposits. The minimum amount required was £50,000. Many with accounts in false names or illegitimate non-resident accounts fell into this category. NIB head office knew the identity of some of these people. Their identity would have been noted when requests for credit on their behalf had been made. Their hidden accounts would not normally be included on credit application forms but a detachable note was usually added. This note would point out that the net worth of the applicant was greater than that suggested by the form. It would refer to any non-resident or false name account held on behalf of the customer. Obviously customers of this type could be very amenable to the offshore scheme.

A meeting was typically set up between a representative of FASD and the customer. This could take place at the local bank branch, or in the homes or offices of the potential investors. Sometimes the branch manager would make the introduction. Other times the investment advisers would act alone.

The administration fees were expensive. One NIB source confirmed that in all the cases he was aware of, the money invested was lodged back on deposit in a numbered account in the NIB branch from which it had come. The rate of interest earned on deposit was the same as if it had never been 'transferred' offshore. The source added that investors were given easy access to their money over the counter at their local NIB branch. When money was taken out over the counter, the bank had to inform CMI to make administrative adjustments at their end. It was all a bit crude, and it became quite tricky to manage. Eventually it was centralised in Dublin and tightened up a little. The investors, however, maintained easy access to their money. There would be no gain for the investors—except to have a numbered account.

A relatively small number of NIB employees had marketed the scheme in the early 1990s. It took a few phone calls to get all their names and the details of where they were now.

Industry sources considered the administrative charges for the CMI product to be huge. Investors had to pay almost 10% in charges to put their money into the scheme. The CMI product was not even authorised for sale in this country. CMI is based in the Isle of Man, which is not part of the European Union.

Under Irish insurance law, you cannot sell an insurance product from an organisation based outside the EU without authorisation from the Government. NIB had no such authorisation.

The CMI link had proved very lucrative for National Irish Bank staff. CMI brought sales people on luxury incentive trips, but only when they achieved a very high level of sales. The trips were to places like Bangkok and Australia, first-class flights and hotels. All expenses were paid, and partners and spouses were included.

Two of the investors we spoke to had not declared their original monies to the Revenue Commissioners. The investors admitted their money had previously been lodged in non-resident accounts. Both had also made it clear that executives from the bank had sought them out and invited them into the scheme.

We have bank letters that refer to a wealthy businessman from the Cork region. He had more than half a million pounds stashed in NIB under a false name. In September 1993 he met with a branch manager from another part of the country and an investment adviser from the FASD. They convinced him to invest in the CMI scheme. Five months later, however, the businessman had a change of heart. He decided to avail of the 1993 Government tax amnesty. He took his money back from CMI. When he discovered he had been charged £45,000 in charges for a five-month investment, he had a really big row with NIB. Letters and memos about this dispute were exchanged internally within the bank.

NIB had been paid £18,000 by CMI for convincing this Cork-based customer to invest in the offshore scheme. We have copies of lodgment and withdrawal slips related to the Cork businessman's investment. They show the businessman made the mistake of signing his real name on the bottom of one of the withdrawal slips. He then had to sign his false name beside it. Other internal correspondence in our possession confirms that NIB had a sum of the order of £30 million in investments with CMI at that stage.

The Government tax amnesty was announced in May 1993. Anyone wishing to avail of it had to do so by the middle of January 1994. These letters and these slips prove the bank knowingly targeted someone they knew was evading tax, five months after the amnesty was announced. They knew it was a false name account held in a branch very far from where the customer operated his main business. The bank could never claim to be ignorant of his situation.

The internal bank paperwork shows clearly that NIB knowingly invited a tax evader to put his money back on deposit in a numbered account in their bank at a time when it was clearly illegal to do so. NIB had a legal obligation to tell the likes of this investor to come clean. Yet instead, they went out of their way to encourage him to put his money into the scheme, right under the nose of the Revenue Commissioners.

Other aspects of the internal paperwork were also worth noting. For instance, we were struck by how much NIB had bent over backwards to appease the businessman for fear he might take his deposit elsewhere. We were struck also by the fact that NIB earned £18,000 for convincing its own customer to put money 'offshore', despite holding on to the money themselves. With revenue like this to be had, the bank obviously had a big incentive to push the scheme hard. There was also the fact that CMI had charged the investor £45,000 for a five-month investment of just over £0.5 million. Who in their right mind would pay such a large fee to put their own money in the exact same type of bank account it was originally invested in, knowing it would earn the exact same rate of interest it was originally earning?

Core of the scandal

NIB's claim that the personal tax implications of the scheme had nothing to do with the bank, but was an issue for the investors themselves, is untrue. According to our tax legislation, it has been a criminal offence since 1982 for anyone knowingly to assist a person to evade taxes. Our investigation centered on the fact that it was NIB who ensured that the money invested in the scheme was brought back to its branches. This was the core of the scandal. If this couldn't be proven, the whole story would have fallen apart.

CMI said the decision on how the funds were actually invested depended totally on the relationship between the investor and his investment manager. NIB acted as the investment manager for all of its customers. This meant it was NIB who decided, in conjunction with its customers, exactly how the money should be invested. CMI never gave any advice to the purchaser of a Personal Portfolio bond in relation to the management of their funds. According to a CMI spokesman: 'The Personal Portfolio product sold to NIB customers was termed 'whole of life.' It was not a fixed term investment. It could effectively run until the investor died. However, there was no lock-in period. The investors could withdraw some, or all, of their money at any time. Where the money was invested was entirely a matter decided between the investor and National Irish Bank.'

The script for our first television report read as follows:

> Prior to 1994, representatives of National Irish Bank gathered information in relation to about 180 of its customers throughout the country. These included people who held non-resident accounts, accounts in false names and accounts with funds which had not been disclosed to the Revenue Commissioners … The money was handed over by bank draft to Clerical Medical International (CMI) in the Isle of Man. Within days, this money, minus the set-up charges, came back to National

Irish Bank ... The bank was able to retain on its balance sheet most of the funds belonging to the holders of the accounts involved and also earned sizeable commissions from Clerical Medical International for selling the bonds ... (NIB) was paid close to £20,000 in commission for persuading a customer to invest half a million pounds ... in excess of 150 National Irish Bank customers accepted the bank's invitation to invest in the CMI bonds ... a customer cashed in his bond to avail of the tax amnesty in early 1994 ... in August 1994 the total amount still invested through the scheme was of the order of £30 million ... National Irish Bank has told RTE that it does not condone tax evasion and, following our enquiries, is conducting an on-going investigation.

In responding to our report, the bank did not even threaten or hint at taking legal action against Charlie Bird, myself or RTE.

Under the provisions of the 1994 Criminal Justice Act, a bank is obliged to report to the police a suspicion that any entity it supervises has committed or is committing the offence of money laundering. Money laundering in this context embraces tax evasion. To our eyes, NIB's first detailed statement about CMI, issued on 29 January 1998, confirmed almost all aspects of the story we had broadcast about CMI. In its statement, however, National Irish Bank finally admitted that it encouraged its customers to appoint NIB as their investment adviser. The bank also admitted that it encouraged its customers to put their money back on deposit in their local NIB branch.

The issue of how easy it had been for customers to get at their money, once invested in the scheme, appeared to be clouded. At one point in the statement, the bank claimed that investors were not entitled to direct access to their funds. At another stage, it claimed that part of the reason for ensuring customer funds were re-lodged in NIB was to make it accessible for encashment purposes. The bank also went on to admit that shortcomings were identified in the administration of the scheme in 1994 and that, as a result, all the deposits were moved to a central location.

Revenue laws dating from 1982 make it clear that aiding and abetting a person to evade tax is a criminal offence. If caught, an individual faces a fine of £1,000 and/or one year in prison for each offence under summary conviction. If the case goes before a jury, the penalty rises to £10,000 and/or ten years in prison for every person assisted.

The advantages of the scheme as marketed were as follows:

- no customer name on any account;
- no probate required in case of death;
- easy accessibility of the funds;

- and the exact same deposit account and interest rate as the client already had.

A 9% fee charged on the portfolio was unavoidable. Every investor had to pay it whether in for five weeks, five months or five years. The bank charged wealthy individuals this fee of 9% to replace the name on their bank accounts with a number. NIB have stated that they actively encouraged investors to use this option. Why would they openly market such an expensive option if they did not at least suspect the investor was a tax evader?

One investor from Cork (now deceased) described for us how he had several bogus non-resident accounts and one day received a phone call from his NIB branch. The manager arranged to come and see him at his workplace. An NIB investment sales person and one of the bank's investment advisers arrived with him. They brought a range of charts and reports and delivered a lengthy presentation. They pushed him to sign up for the scheme but the businessman objected because of the scale of the fees. He said he couldn't believe it was so expensive and yet offered no interest rate advantage over the accounts he already had. Bank insiders told us the product was specifically targeted at people with bogus non-resident accounts. The re-lodging of offshore monies into an Irish deposit account offered no advantage to legitimate savers.

NIB typically employed very aggressive national and local marketing and advertising techniques when launching new products. This did not happen for the CMI personal portfolio, however. It appears to have been sold under the counter to customers who fitted a specific description.

Special savings accounts with a low 10% rate of DIRT (Deposit Interest Retention Tax) had been introduced in the 1993 budget. A married couple with £100,000 to invest legitimately could put their money into a special savings account for five years provided they made a declaration to the Revenue Commissioners. This would be subject to the 10% rate of DIRT per year on the interest earned instead of the typical DIRT rate of 27% at that stage. If the rate of return or interest earned on the deposit worked out also at 10% per year, the couple would end up with £154,000 net of tax after five years and there would be no remaining tax liability. But if they had invested in the CMI offshore scheme as promoted and encouraged by NIB, they would end up with £149,000 gross after the five years (i.e. £5,000 less) and still face an additional tax bill of £6,000 for DIRT. In net terms they would be £10,000 worse off. Encouraging legitimate investors to avail of this CMI / NIB option defied logic. NIB boldly admitted in a public statement that it was its policy to actively encourage its offshore investors to ensure their funds were re-deposited back at their local NIB branch.

At one point, I estimated that NIB earned over £1 million in commission from selling CMI personal portfolios and that CMI earned over £3 million for investments it did not even manage. My figures also suggested that the Irish Exchequer had lost about £26.5 million as a result of the scheme. That was enough to cut 1% off the top rate of income tax on budget day at the height of the scheme.

Another scandal

The effect of the National Irish Bank offshore investment story was phenomenal. There was a considerable element of follow-up from the newspapers and other media. It immediately resulted in our receiving more documentation, including internal audit reports from within National Irish Bank. These internal audit reports revealed another scandal. But this new scandal was even more shocking. The reports showed that the bank, in addition to operating the CMI scheme, had been deducting money from people's bank accounts for years 'without permission and for no legitimate reason.'

The impact of this new information was explosive for the financial industry. It caused a major public re-assessment on the part of many members of the public about the position of bankers in our society. Official investigations directly into the events on behalf of the public are still going on to this day. There have also been other knock-on effects. After the NIB affair, we were approached by an individual who had key information and documentation about Allied Irish Banks' (AIB) alleged 53,000 bogus non-resident accounts. In the end, that person chose to go the *Sunday Independent* with the information but it was clear that it was our NIB story that had provoked him to come forward. That information resulted in a major parliamentary investigation into tax evasion throughout the banking industry, going back to the late 1980s. New legislation was invoked to enable the Oireachtas (Parliament) Public Accounts Committee to compel the country's top bankers to publicly answer questions under oath about the extent to which their organization assisted customers in tax evasion. The enquiry also examined the failure of the banks to live up to their obligations in operating the Deposit Income Retention Tax (DIRT) for over a decade. The DIRT enquiry, as it was called, resulted in a major shake-up of the entire financial services industry. For bankers, accountants, tax advisers and others, business would never be the same again.

In excess of £200 million has so far accrued to the State as a direct result of the various investigations sparked off by the initial phone call to the RTE newsroom in January 1998. In addition, procedures throughout the financial industry have, in many respects, been completely revolutionised. The way in which the Central Bank regulates the financial services sector has also been transformed and the Central Bank itself is being re-organised and re-constituted as a result.

The National Irish Bank story and the way it happened reflects the fact that Irish journalism has shifted. A new combination of specialist reporters, and the way they are being mixed in with generalist reporters, is bringing about a new style of journalism. And when one looks at ongoing tribunals of inquiry into practices in other areas of public life, it seems that this new era in journalism will last for a considerable period of time.

The way we uncovered the National Irish Bank scandal is a perfect example of this mix at work. I consider myself to be a specialist reporter of economic and financial affairs. But in the NIB case I was faced with a generalist reporter in the shape of Charlie Bird coming to me and saying, 'I met some guy in a car park and he gave me these pages. What do they mean?' And so, for the next three or four months, I was launched into a virtual whirlwind of investigative journalism. For twenty-four hours a day, seven days a week, we chased up those pages, learning what that offshore scheme was about, and learning about the illegitimate deductions from customer accounts. Huge changes have resulted from taking Charlie Bird's generalist approach to journalism and marrying it with my specialist approach. It was a potent mix and produced something that really had an impact.

Budget 2000

Budget 2000 was one of the biggest economic stories of recent years and it is one that I fear I will never be able to forget. It was a story, or perhaps even an event, that brought home to me how important it is to stand back at times from all the positive economic news of recent years and consider where we are going as a society.

In the run-up to Budget 2000, I had no reason to expect any unusual policy changes to be announced. I had previously done live RTE broadcasts on eight budgets so I knew the run of the mill. I knew about the state of the Government's finances. I knew about Government commitments in relation to the social partnership agreement between the Government, unions and employers, and the necessity to lay the groundwork for a new social partnership deal. The Government had a very large surplus, so there was a lot of spare money. There was a commitment to the European Commission that the Exchequer would not put too much money into the economy for fear of causing inflation. The possible changes in the budget appeared to have been well signalled. The previous year, in Budget 1999, the Government had introduced tax credits. That was a very radical move in my view. It reflected a decision—I saw it as a decision—that, in future, the fruits of economic growth, or at least that proportion of them that accrue, to the Exchequer, would be divided equally among taxpayers. Tax credits could ensure that everybody would benefit equally from any future increase in tax-free allowance. Everybody would get the same increase in take-home pay.

Budget 2000 was different. I expected, and I think that most people would have expected, that the Government would follow through with the tax credit policies of Budget 1999. I had no idea of what was about to happen or the shock that was in store for me and for most other observers.

Two days before the budget, I interviewed the Finance Minister, Charlie McCreevy. He spoke a lot about social inclusion and said he would lift people out of the tax net. There was no surprise to me in any of that, given the amount of spare money at his disposal.

Then the Minister stood up to deliver his speech on budget day. I was all geared up for one of the biggest giveaway budgets ever delivered, a purely good news story. And that's how it started out. That was also how it was presented and received in the Dáil by his Government party colleagues.

Individualisation

But as the Minister read through his speech, I was struck by the one sentence where he spoke about the individualisation of income tax bands. It involved an increase in tax bands for individuals of £6,000, of £12,000 for two-income families, but by nothing whatsoever for single-income family couples. The Minister called it the 'individualisation of tax bands' and then carried on. It was very well received at that time by people on the Government side of the benches.

But as I sat considering his sentence and the details of what he had announced, the hair on the back of my neck stood up. It was an instant reaction. This was no ordinary budget. This individualisation process had the potential to change the way we run our families, the way we run our lives. Perhaps this is something that any Government minister is entitled to do. But it seems reasonable to expect at least a warning. It seems reasonable to have expected some discussion or debate beforehand about the merits of such a major change. It seems reasonable to have expected that the Government may have included such a proposal in its election manifesto so it would have received a mandate for such a major change. It seems reasonable for the public to have been given some context for such a change. But none of these things had occurred at any stage in advance of the budget. The individualisation of the tax bands in Budget 2000 came as a complete shock to me and to everybody else. How was I going to explain to the general public in a short television broadcast what this measure meant?

The details of the budget showed the plan was to spend £840 million on this particular style of individualised tax break over three years. Yet not a single penny of that enormous amount of money would go to single-income families. The plan was to ensure that a single-income family would pay the same tax rate as the super rich once their family income hit £28,000 but that a double-income family could earn up to £56,000 before hitting the super-rich rate.

I had a very short period of time before I went live on air and I toyed around with how I would explain it. I will never forget that broadcast. As I went on air I was battling to restrain myself, acutely aware of the requirement through the

Broadcasting Act to be fair and balanced. In this instance, it was going to be most difficult to strike that balance.

Live on air, I was asked the question as to what was in the budget. My answer started by saying it was pretty poor for the low-paid. I said I was very surprised at how much money was being spent, and at how little the low-paid would receive. The well-paid and well-off had done very well out of the tax changes introduced.

Then I moved on to the individualisation proposal, which I said was perhaps the most controversial element of the budget, particularly in the way it treated single-income families. My words were: 'The Minister is talking about individualisation of tax bands. Individualisation of society is something which the British had for many years. They called it "Thatcherism" and they got pretty sick of it.' That went way beyond the usual interpretation of a budget, but then this was way beyond a usual budget.

I concluded my broadcast by saying: 'This budget does very many good things … but it is going to remain controversial for a very long time to come because it gave so little to the low-paid and because of the way it treated single-income families.'

I still believe my three-minute analysis was right and that I presented an accurate assessment of the implications of the budget, given the short period of time I had available. Mine were strong words, delivered with a tone to match. In delivering them, I was very much aware of the nature of my audience—a very broad range of people. I needed to portray the budget changes in a way that was relevant for the majority of people. I needed to use words and terminology that got the importance of the tax changes across in no uncertain terms. I believe I succeeded in that, because I have been told that the telephone switchboard in Dáil Éireann lit up as soon as the 6pm television news broadcast was finished and the backlash, which within a week led to the re-balancing of Budget 2000, took off from there.

I don't believe that my broadcast caused the trouble. All I did was to focus people's attention on the issues they needed to think about. I didn't ask anybody to ring up Dáil Éireann and complain. I simply analysed what was in the budget. Mine was an economic report delivered through a public service medium that hit on the central issues in the budget, namely that the low-paid did not do very well out of it, and that there was a really important feature in the tax changes which might affect the way we go about organising our families and society in the future. The measures announced by the Minister were striking and surprising, especially given all the pre-budget talk about increasing social inclusion.

When one hears a Government say its aim is have 80% of people paying tax at the standard rate, it is important to look behind the sound-bite and consider precisely which 80% the Government means. The individualisation plan would have had taxpayers who were supporting spouses and large numbers of children, paying income tax at the same rate as millionaires, while single people with no dependents, and families with double incomes, got to divide nearly £1 billion of tax breaks between them. Very serious choices had been made and presented to society without any discussion, debate or proper mandate.

It is important to make financial reporting relevant to ordinary people and to ensure that it is not presented as a specialist subject. Everybody pays taxes. Everybody is entitled to have a family and children, to be single and to make money. So the budget ought to be presented in a fashion that is not just for economists or tax experts. It's for everybody. But to get the message across to people in that fashion, one has to take risks with the words and tone that are used. I believe I took those risks in covering Budget 2000 and I would probably take them again.

Conclusion

What happened during the Budget 2000 coverage probably reflected what happened in my own development: getting to the point where I now accept that I am a broadcast journalist rather than an economist, and accepting that what we do as journalists is important. That's not something I really believed ten years ago when I was being indoctrinated into the culture of economic secrecy so deeply ingrained in my former bosses at the Central Bank.

Not long after my period working for the Central Bank, I moved to the *Sunday Business Post*. It was in the early days of that newspaper, which was instrumental in moving economics and financial reporting from the business pages of Irish newspapers to the front pages. Irish economic and financial journalism has now changed for the good. It is firmly established on the front pages and is set to continue as a force to be reckoned with.

There are more constraints in public service broadcasting than in newspapers. That's not because newspapers are trying to do anything differently, but because newspaper journalists can use more words. They can elaborate and give much more background. Very often in broadcast news there has to be an edge and, without such an edge, people are less inclined to listen. When reporting about a specialist subject in a newspaper or a magazine, you can afford to write for the experts. But in a public service broadcasting organisation like RTE where your listeners are everybody—the widest possible audience you can get—you can less afford to use specialist words. You've got to use a terminology that everybody understands. And you've got to use a tone that will enable people to understand and grasp the importance and meaning of what you are trying to communicate. Sometimes you've got to convey a sense of urgency, not because you've got so little time, but to help portray an element of shock if that is what is required. Perhaps not everyone understands these constraints, but I do believe that economic and financial reporting as a public service does require a broadcast journalist to take some risks.

Aid at a cost: the media and international humanitarian interventions

THIERRY GARCIN

International humanitarian interventions have really been taking place only since the onset of the modern type of international upheaval, that is to say, since about 1990. Such interventions were really new, both in the humanitarian and in the juridical fields. Some years earlier (in the mid and late 1980s), French jurists from universities, such as Mario Bettati, and French doctors from non-governmental organisations, such as Bernard Kouchner and Rony Brauman, developed a doctrine which tended to promote discretionary interventions for humanitarian reasons, backed by military resources and eventually made without any authorisation from the United Nations. The need to avert 'disaster' (whether humanitarian, technological, economic or even 'political'— this last one being rather poorly defined) was offered as a justification for this kind of 'charity at all costs'.

The media played a key role in this development, in increasing public awareness and in sensitising people as to what was going on. As Dr Kouchner once said, with unintended cynicism: 'There is no great disaster without large press coverage.' The nuclear accident in Chernobyl (1986), the earthquake in Soviet Armenia (1988), the collapse of the Ceausescu regime in Rumania (1989), the large scale massacres by Ethiopian Colonel Mengistu of his own population (especially the Christians) followed by famine (1990), contributed to popularise this doctrine in the media and in western societies. Charitable efforts backed by military resources were deemed justified by the compelling need and the appalling television pictures. These disasters had three factors in common:

- the humanitarian emergency took precedence over political considerations or implications;
- the press was a willing but compulsory ally;
- being there was as important as effective intervention.

In considering these ten years (1990-2000) of UN peace-keeping operations and of humanitarian military interventions (some sanctioned by the United Nations, others not), what can we say about the conduct of journalists in such situations? Could we say that the press in general and journalists as individuals

83

were aware of their influence on public opinion, were liable for the damage they caused and deserve censure for their lack of ethical behaviour? These questions are important as, even if the nature of international problems has changed, the press still plays a major role.

On the one hand, UN peace-keeping operations are no longer in vogue (indeed, they have diminished in quantity and quality). On the other, states and governments are tending to avoid getting stuck in humanitarian interventions (in the Democratic Republic of Congo from 1997 to 2000; in East Timor in 1999). In fact, the present apathy towards the continuing Turkish interventions in Iraq (and also in Iran), the illegal Anglo-American air bombings in Iraq, the occupation of a large part of Azerbaijan by Armenia and of ex-Zaire by their neighbours, the NATO 'war' against the new Yugoslavia without any UN reso-lution, and so on, clearly show that military interventions are becoming more widely accepted and tolerated by tired western public opinion. Humanitarian values are gradually being transformed into humanitarian indifference, and this despite UN Secretary General Kofi Annan's solemn promotion of the merits of international humanitarian interventions (that is to say, the right to intervene by force in the internal affairs of another state).

Given this evolution, we might ask, 'Have the media also been stood down?' Four examples will help us to re-evaluate the situation and to 'judge'—with the frankness of friendship—the activities of our much-vaunted western journalists.

Iraq, 1991

The 1991 Gulf War lasted five weeks, in which, because of the systematic and invisible night-time air-raids, television could show nothing apart from five days of land fights against exhausted Iraqi soldiers. For five months after the Gulf War, the standard of news was so poor that journalists were reduced to filming themselves on the roofs of Riyadh or Dhahran hotels, 'clogging up the airwaves'. After this the United Nations authorised a military intervention on behalf of certain communities (Kurds and Shiites) persecuted by Baghdad. The pertinent resolution (688) urged help for *all* who needed assistance throughout *all* Iraq. Not surprisingly, absolutely nothing was done to alleviate the disas-trous situation in which the Shiite community found themselves. But, in addi-tion, absolutely nothing was done by the media to remind their public of the half-hearted implementation of this resolution. The Kurdish situation, on the other hand, was covered in a sensational and reckless manner. The result was that one tragedy was forgotten because of the type of focus on the other. This situation was not as implausible as it sounds, since the media were totally unaware of the UN resolution. Also, European public opinion had made up its mind as to where its duties lay: as we had been benevolent to the Kurdish pop-ulation, we thought the Kurdish problem would be solved sooner or later, and so perhaps were more inclined to want to be part of the success.

Somalia, 1992–1993

In 1992, having failed in his bid for re-election, George Bush's presidency was in its twilight. Moved by the sight of starvation on television—in particular the famine that was killing children—or by American public opinion (which probably could not locate Mogadishu on a map), he decided to intervene militarily by means of a UN resolution (794), which called for, in a surrealist exhortation, a 'political settlement'. Many will recall the cameramen welcoming the first units as they landed on the beach. As it happened, in France and perhaps in other European countries, despite the tragic circumstances, this piece of film quickly became the subject of humour and mockery (perhaps misplaced).

We should bear in mind that, for the opposite or reverse reasons, the United States quickly abandoned its intervention: the American public was distraught when it saw its GIs or marines wounded, or their bodies dragged through the streets as an additional humiliation. This did not prevent Washington from negotiating with the local warlords, and it did not prevent European public opinion from leaving the Somali people to their fate. Today, who cares about the *de facto* partition of that country?

This case illustrates in stark terms the contradictions of both politics and media, especially the danger of approaching problems with an excess of self-confidence. Perhaps 'decency' should be the first and last word in any discussion of media accountability.

Rwanda, 1994

Even if journalists worked too closely with military forces and non-governmental organisations, the press coverage of what was essentially a French intervention (only 500 African soldiers were involved) was satisfactory both from an ethical and a professional point of view (there was no concentration on gruesome details). The coverage, however, was open to criticism because of the use of uncorroborated and exaggerated figures—one million deaths; the transformation of Tutsis into angelic fighters, etc.

Nevertheless, this difficult operation (named 'Turquoise'), authorised by a UN resolution (929), gave rise to serious controversy concerning former political actions and responsibilities of successive French Governments. So much so that Paris was sometimes harshly accused of having been involved in the aircrash in which the Presidents of Rwanda and Burundi both died. Although these charges or rumours were absurd—what would have been the advantage to Paris in killing the leader of a friendly regime?—they were widely commented on in newspapers and in the broadcast media, mainly because they came in part from a Belgian journalist.

Last but not least, crucial regional background information was nearly always forgotten: the clear anti-democratic behaviour of the new regime in Kigali; the cowardice of the Organisation for African Unity during and after the genocide;

the reluctance of African heads of state to intervene (they did not want to do what could one day be done to them). Once again, the day-to-day coverage of the humanitarian operation meant that important geopolitical consequences were omitted or hidden. Also, young reporters in the field often came directly from the news desk and had very poor knowledge of the history of the country or the region.

The opposite mistake was made later on, out of laziness or incompetence, when self-appointed President Kabila of what was formerly Zaire, helped by a pro-American alliance (from Eritrea and Ethiopia, to Angola and Namibia), came into power in a bloodbath so blatant that a UN document compared it to a 'crime against humanity'. In this case the humanitarian dimension was ignored as the focus was on the possible political consequences: the risk of massive upheaval in Central Africa. American newspapers were never fond of such thorough investigations, while in Europe today they often play a leading moral role, although in a rather detached manner.

Liberia, 1990–1997
If the Somalian conflict received excessive coverage by western media, the tribal and ethnic war in Liberia was of no interest at all to European journalists. Nevertheless, the conflict was long and cruel, and the international ramifications were considerable. The region is at the crossroads between French-speaking and English-speaking areas. American forces liberated western citizens, French-speaking countries (Ivory Coast) were involved in the war, and Nigeria commanded a regional force (ECOWAS) sent by a regional organisation on behalf of the United Nations.

Although children became soldiers overnight and even warriors or torturers, although war spread over Sierra Leone in a predictable way, although the intensity of violence and the amount of constant horrors (including systematic amputations) were huge in Sierra Leone, it is striking how both Liberian and Sierra-Leonese conflicts were nearly forgotten in the French press. Neither conflict received regular meaningful coverage. The Sierra-Leonese war was in fact 'rediscovered' in 1999, just as it was ending. Perhaps this was as a result of remorse, or of an effort to try to make up. Better late than never, but a pity all the same.

French media coverage
In France, this political misperception of international humanitarian interventions was increased for several reasons that had to do with the profession of journalism itself.

There is no charter of rights and duties for journalists, except one short text published by a trade union body in 1918 (just before the end of World War 1) and amended in 1938. Its precepts are vague and several are obsolete. Some were never applied due to a lack of *ad hoc* structures. Several were modernised in a charter of rights published in Frankfurt in 1971 by relevant European organisations. There is no Press Council as in England, even though specialists keep proposing an entity of this type every twenty years to so, but with little conviction. The prospect of such a professional body would cause alarm among newspaper owners and editors, who immediately reject it as being inspired by a 'Vichyist' or 'Petainist' vision of corporations. Meanwhile, the tendency is to establish elementary rules in some TV channels and newspapers, and to adapt them (even though they are not often implemented) according to the type of audience in question.

Of course, in the context of this chapter's topic, this lack of ethical structures or professional bodies is not the main concern (see endnote). What is much more important, what is in fact the crucial point, is the general professional atmosphere in which journalists live and work. Just like non-governmental organisations in international humanitarian interventions, they are fascinated by the culture of urgency: news of any kind is supposed to be broadcast immediately in a shortened and imperious news cycle. But, when everything is urgent, nothing is urgent, and then reality ceases to matter. This often provokes a 'reality' deficit.

It's not so easy to propose an optimum way of improving the situation in practice, especially among television networks. The effect of round-the-clock news channels is a complicating factor. In addition, television images have an inordinate influence on an emotionally-susceptible and captive public opinion, an influence that has knock-on effects on radio news as well as on what we call in France 'regional' newspapers (but which are written and read for 'local' reasons). We also have to reckon with television news presented as cartoons (though, fortunately, things are improving on the specialised news channels), and the fact that the internet is constantly relaying both accurate and inaccurate news indiscriminately, and without real professional expertise, except in the case of on-line newspapers. All these problems lead to an increasing indifference in public opinion towards foreign topics and disaster situations: the intervention in East Timor and the floods in Venezuela were good examples. Overall, it does not augur well for a speedy improvement.

Journalists are at fault, not so much because they do not respect some particular guidelines or some magic rules, but because their state of mind weakens their common sense. We are left to hope that the world-wide and clearly exaggerated discredit that falls on the media as a whole will in the long-term promote a strong reaction. But can we be sure that, as matters stand, this hope is not some kind of wishful thinking?

Endnote: French-speaking readers, if interested, may wish to refer to the following publications by the author:

'La désinformation soviétique', *Défense nationale*, October 1986.
'Terrorisme et medias', *Défense nationale*, May 1987.
'La manoeuvre médiatique dans les interventions outre-mer', *Défense nationale*, December 1989.
'Déontologie des journalistes et exercice de la responsabilité', *Franco-British Studies*, 9
    (Spring 1990).
'La coalition des médias', in "La guerre du Golfe", *Stratégique*, 51, 52 (Fondation pour les études de
    défense nationale, 1991).
'Information et défense' (dossier), *Défense*, 66, December 1994.
'L'intervention française au Rwanda', *Le Trimestre du monde*, 34:2 (1996).
'L'événement internationale et les médias', *Défense nationale*, October 1997.
'Médiatisation versus médiation', *Agir*, 2, December 1999.

Making a difference

MAGGIE O'KANE

International reporting has changed in many ways since I began in the business ten years ago—at least three of them for the worst. Firstly, it has become more dangerous; secondly, it is more controlled by the authorities since the invention of the 'pool system'; and thirdly, the quality of what is produced has been hit by the volume of output demanded.

In the last ten years, conflicts have become increasingly difficult to cover and probably more dangerous—something like 12 journalists died in Vietnam compared to over 30 in Bosnia. In the recent war in Chechnya, most news organisations decided it was simply too dangerous to send reporters because of the hostility of the Russian army and the sheer volume of bombs being pumped into the country.

While admitting to more danger, there is also a problem with the risks factor: the large corporations and management are refusing to let their reportérs go into the field. Instead, TV is relying more and more on Associated Press and Reuters TV who will get the pictures at any cost. But how reliable are their sources? Is the reporting undermined by not having your own people on the ground? For months in Kosovo, the best we could do was allege that atrocities were going on: they were, but we weren't there.

If we are not prepared to take risks anymore, should we be doing the job of foreign correspondent, which is seen as the most glamorous in the newspaper cupboard? Is there not a case to be made for giving up the seat to a paying passenger?

I sometimes look at this job as that of a 'fireman'. As special correspondents, we are often called firemen. Firstly, we usually volunteer for the job and, like firemen, we do have a duty to stick around when the going gets tough. This is difficult. I know myself that I survived for only five days in Chechnya because I felt too scared and vulnerable to stay on. But there is a growing tendency nowadays for a rapid exodus. Timor was an example. In East Timor after the elections, it was incredibly important that journalists stay behind. But there was intimidation and, after a BBC reporter had his arm broken, there was a mass exodus from the capital, Dili, led by the TV networks. In fact only three reporters stayed behind, all of them women, including Marie Colvin of the *Sunday Times*, who probably helped change the course of events there.

The annoying thing about the exodus was that, as each TV crew pulled out, they took with them the up-links and the means to get the pictures out. No attempt was made to try and find arrangements so that those who were committed to staying would have some way to get the pictures out. There was more concern about saving the valuable kit than getting the pictures of what was shaping up to be, and what could have been without women like Marie Colvin's commitment to reporting, a massacre.

'Making a difference' is the title of this chapter. Some people may indeed smile. But the United Nations had sent an order from New York in mid-September for an evacuation of the UN compound in Dili, leaving behind all the people who had fled there for shelter. This may sound familiar—remember Srebenica. The order caused a revolt among a small group of UN staff and, with the help of Marie Colvin, who was broadcasting everywhere by satellite telephone and reinforcing the message that the UN was yet again preparing to abandon these people, the decision was rescinded.

That was good news from Timor. But look at Chechnya. What is happening there makes Sarajevo in its worst days seem easy. Chechnya is being covered from Moscow on the basis of handouts from the Russian Ministry of Information and from the border at Inghusetia, where the story dried up at Christmas 1999 when the refugees stopped coming.

Yes, Chechnya is terribly dangerous and also most violent: the largest scale bombing of a city since the Second World War. It deserves to be leading the news every night. The scale of the destruction and the indiscriminate nature of it is something I've never seen before in my lifetime. Yet, not a single international news organisation is anywhere near the place. News managers are reluctant to take decisions to send their own people, or even to look for volunteers. Instead, TV exploits freelance camera men and women without even crediting them.

How many times have you seen ITV and BBC pictures coming from inside Grozny, supplied by the extremely brave or extremely desperate freelancers, without even being credited. In Grozny during the last war, the rumours were that the pictures were being shot by young boys who were given a video camera and $100 dollars a day and told to get on with it.

My point is that, over the last ten years, the speed at which crews, particularly television crews, are ordered to evacuate, is leaving us without any really responsible coverage. My argument, I suppose, is that when you find people who are prepared to do the job, then pay them properly and back them up properly. War correspondents must do their duty, just as volunteer firemen must do theirs.

The second reason why the job of foreign reporting is going down the tubes is the famous, odious pool. In the Vietnam war, they were forever jumping on and off 'Hueys', but by the time the Falkland war came, they had invented the 'pool' system. Here, a certain number of selected journalists are allowed to go, with the idea that they will report back to the others. It is the godsend of governments, military authorities and shady dealers. It diminishes the energy of journalists by leaving them squabbling among themselves. It has become all-pervasive and it makes me shudder every time I hear mention of the pool. It's as though every press relations officer's first lesson starts with the merits of the pool. The other drawback to it is that what has been lined up for 'the pool' is invariably boring—a press officer's idea of what journalists should report in war is, I hope, different to what journalists feel they ought to cover.

The pool system had its origins in Vietnam when the US administrations of Kennedy and Johnston realised that the war had been a public relations disaster because the media roamed and reported freely. In the Falklands, the limitations on accommodation on ships cruising out to the war-zone ensured that the military could pick and choose who went. It seemed like a perfect system. In the Gulf War, it was implemented enthusiastically by all the major allied forces. There were four standard stories: 'Our boys arriving in the desert; sending letters home; girls joining the boys; and the camp cook.' 'That was it,' said one US producer, 'that's what we got to cover.'

It is however a system that suits some of the lazier styles of journalism. It ensures that everyone's back is covered and everyone gets the story—if it is a story. In Kurdistan, it reduced journalists to squabbling among themselves and ratting on each other. That was in 1991. In Timor at the end of 1999, we found ourselves spending day after day ensuring that we were on the airlift to Timor: negotiating the pool was much more exhausting that actually reporting what was going on. That is the tyranny of television: it brings out the worst in us all. Bolshie TV producers—and sometimes the women are the worst: chummy chaps buying drinks for boring military press officers, while the younger among us gaze dolefully into their eyes.

Truly, truly sad. Divisive and energy sapping. I actually decided that I would prefer to go into Kosovo with the UN troops, across the Albanian border, because that operation was being run by the Germans and they had no experience of international forces' operations and of 'handling' the press. I was right: they let us run around, but when you strayed down the wrong road, some pimply Italian would tell you that you couldn't pass. I have come close to physical violence very few times in my life, but it was usually when dealing with the military—the ones on our side.

That, perhaps, is why some of the most astonishing and best stuff comes from those journalists who are committed to leaving the pool behind. I've just finished reading Fergal Keane's book, *Rivers of Blood*. That, I have to say, is how it should be done. Keane, his producer, and camera and sound man, went it alone to investigate the Rwandan genocide. They crisscrossed the country, uncovering massacres and looking for the perpetrators. Having been through

the 1999 wars in Kosovo, Timor and Chechnya, and having seen the big corporations at work, I really doubt that Fergal Keane would have been allowed to
go around alone, as he was in Rwanda in 1994. For example, only three cameras made it into Kosovo through Serb lines, and they were all freelancers.

But shouldn't viewers be horrified if that's what it takes to force change?
Can you imagine the suffering going on in Grozny? I'm sure there are news-
managers in basements deciding not to show pictures coming out without
anaesthetics. The fact that Russia has been given such an easy ride by the international community is because, unlike Bosnia, we have been spared the TV and
print pictures that force us to make moral and political decisions about what
should be done. Why?—Because all the firemen went home.

The third problem that international correspondents now face is the sheer
volume of reporting that they have to produce, and the effect that has on quality. Since the advent of CNN, and BBC 24-hour news, there have been huge
increases in the number of daily reports, making it almost impossible for many
working in TV and radio to find the time to find something to report on. The
BBC reporter, Jacky Rowlands, services dozens of different outlets: Radio 5,
Radio 4, News 24, Radio One, Radio Scotland—the list is unending. The
arrival of the mobile telephone and the constant calls for unnecessary live
updates make it impossible to do investigative journalism. That makes the journalist more reliant on official government press releases. In this scenario, who-
ever is the most efficient at delivering fax and emails to the journalists, under
siege from their news-desks, may get the best coverage. A truly dangerous
trend.

That brings me to my third point: that so-called god of reporting, 'objectivity'. I have a problem with this word and usually with the kind of people who
keep making an issue of it. I have always had it since Bosnia. To be honest, I
remember doing my first RTE interview for the Sunday radio news programme from the Croatian town of Osijek in 1992. I was unsure whether I was
in a Croat town or a Serb town and whether it was Croats or Serbs who were
attacking. Afterwards my good friend Anne Cassin told me, 'You really did
sound like you were winging that one.'

I had no agenda at the beginning of the Bosnian war. I hardly understood
who was who. I'm not making an argument for ignorance, just proving the
point that I didn't have an agenda. Yet for the first two years of that war, we
journalists were getting it in the face: 'bias', 'Muslim sympathisers'—emotional
and over-reacting because we insisted that the roots of this horror were not
some 'ancient ethnic conflict', the favoured diplomatic phrase of 1992, but a
very modern manipulation of power. So we were heavily criticised. Why?
Because the European political agenda at the time was for non-intervention
and, in order to justify that, there had to be a symmetry of guilt. Everyone went
along with it.

But in November 1999, the stand taken by those journalists who were accused of not being 'objective' was vindicated by the United Nations' apology on Srebrenica when Kofi Annan's report acknowledged that there were aggressors and victims, and that the UN had been wrong to treat the aggressors and the victims in the same way.

I suppose my line on all this is that truth is often not objective, and the people I hear crying and lamenting the loss of objectivity are those who are most uncomfortable with the truth. In Bosnia, that was usually the Serbs or the politicians in Europe who were much more comfortable with casting a neutral 'objective' eye on the situation than with facing the truth which demanded responses that required political and moral judgement.

So let's ditch objectivity in favour of truth. And when it comes to being firemen, we have to get back to climbing up the ladder. This of course may all sound pretty 'gung ho' crap from someone who is thinking about retiring. In my last two wars, in Timor and Chechnya, I came closer to getting killed than I have in the last ten years. In Timor, it was a bullet that came so close that my ear popped. In Chechnya, it involved being chased by a low-flying Russian attack helicopter. All of that has made me reflect very much on my own position, and that I think is fair enough. But my argument is that danger has to be part of the package, that and retirement from this kind of job should mean a clean break. I'm still trying to make up my mind. Is it worth it? Worth what?—What is it? A friend of mine called Corinne Dufka, who has worked for Reuters in most of the dangerous spots of the world, put it simply as: 'making a difference'. And if you're not doing it anymore, then maybe it's time to get off the pot.

And finally, let's end on a good note. Something huge has happened in international affairs, in which we in international media can play a role: the Hague and the Rwanda Human Rights Tribunals. In February 2000, a 46-year-old Rwandan called Tharcisse Muvunyi was arrested in Lewisham in South London on a warrant issued by the Rwanda Tribunal. He faces five counts of genocide and crimes against humanity. He's appealing and protesting his innocence, but it looks as though the alleged commander will, at least, face trial.

In Timor, during a chat with an unusually outspoken and deeply passionate UN official from the UN Human Rights Monitoring Group, I was told that in their meeting with the five Indonesian military chiefs after the violence of the elections, the threat of a Hague-type tribunal had sent a chill through the room. He believed it helped towards a quick capitulation by the generals.

But the greatest spectacle of all has been Pinochet—I do not believe any of this can be underestimated. The *de facto* creation of a permanent war crimes tribunal, and the precedents set by the Pinochet rulings, send an extraordinary message. In Bosnia and Rwanda, they believed they were immune to prosecution, but now the precedent has been established. Also, in Cambodia, the UN is planning to have hearings on the Khmer Rouge.

The work done by journalists to highlight cases such as Muvunyi, who was first tracked by the BBC's 9-o'clock news, is important. I know journalists from Bosnia who are still getting calls from the Hague about reports they wrote on the killers during the worst year of the Bosnian wars.

So take comfort—there is cause for at least some.

Do the poor only come out at Christmas? The media and social exclusion

JOE DUFFY

A t the outset it is worth trying to come up with some definition or under-standing of social exclusion—a relatively new label. If it's new, Tony Blair must have something to do with it. Speaking in December 1997 during a visit to a school in Lambeth in London, he gave the New Labour definition of social exclusion:

> Social exclusion is about income, but it is about much more. It is about prospects and networks and life chances. It is a very modern problem and one that is more harmful to the individual, more damaging to self esteem, more corrosive for society as a whole, more likely to be passed down from generation to generation than material poverty.

What is especially interesting about this definition is the last remark: that social exclusion is more likely to be passed down from generation to generation than poverty.

A task force of the Stockholm HLTT (High Level Think Tank) in 1998 came up with this definition: 'a dynamic process, best described as descending levels; some disadvantages lead to some exclusion, which in turn leads to more disadvantages and more social exclusion, and ends up with persistent multiple deprivation and disadvantages. Individuals, households, and spatial units can be excluded from access to resources like employment, health, education and social or political life. Society recognises social exclusion risk when it accepts that individuals and households are dissatisfied with their current situations and role in society, and are unable to bring about sustainable improvements due to lack of means and confidence and/or because of discrimination.'

Any study of social exclusion should focus at some point on the role of the mass media. Let us remind ourselves of the wonder of the media we work in. Remember that our own medium brings so much information, knowledge, entertainment and joy into our lives and those of almost every single man, woman and child on the island. And let's also remind ourselves that what we produce is welcomed daily by almost everyone in the land, possibly with the

exception at the moment of some bogus non-resident Ansbacher account-hold-
ers.

We work in a wonderful medium, and are treated with great respect—indeed
affection—by such a large proportion of the people. One great feature of our
work is the bridge-building aspect of communication: opening doors, sharing
experiences, questioning the powerful and allowing the powerless access. And
let us not forget the uplift which groups or individuals can get from being
allowed tell their history, make their point or challenge an injustice. There is a
danger that on the day-to-day treadmill we might become blasé. We need to
remember that while politicians breeze in and out of interviews, the powerless
and the marginalized are, by definition, unused to all of this. Basic courtesies,
hospitality, and even a little bit of advice would not go astray. So the points I
wish to make are in this context.

'Middle-classness' of the media

It will not come as a revelation that the media is middle-class. We work, we get
paid, ergo we are catapulted into the marketer's dream segment: the AB category. But that is not a handicap, it is nothing to be ashamed of. That's simply the
way it is. It is as it is, or as Frank Mc Court would say, 'tis'. But we need not be
middle-class by outlook. While our media organisations have a massive national
audience, closer scrutiny shows that we pull in proportionately more middle-
class audiences than working-class. But that should not mean that this is the
only segment of the population we should address.

While in population and percentage terms, radio has a remarkable audience
penetration—only about one in ten Irish people do not listen to the radio on a
given day—in class terms the figure begins to drop as income drops (see Table
1). To take RTE Radio 1 as an example: it has nearly twice the penetration in
the higher social groups than the lower ones, while Today FM reaches only one
in eight of the lower socio-economic groups.

The irony is that while Radio 1 has a public-service remit, i.e., primarily talk
as opposed to music—even though the major part of its income comes from
advertising—the public service remit, it would seem, suits the middle-class
more than the working-class.

Newspapers are different: while approximately one out of every two people
read a morning paper, the social class divide is much more pronounced among
individual titles than among radio stations. Seven times as many people in Bal-
lyfermot read the *Star* as the *Irish Times*—while almost three times as many
people in Foxrock grab a look at the 'paper of record' every day as the afore-
mentioned *Star*.

While radio stations generally have a greater and broader reach than individual newspapers, our mission is to attempt to address a wider audience. It is also

Table 1

Radio stations: national social class reach, July 2000 to June 2001

JNLR/MRBI Survey, July 2000-June 2001 Monday-Friday Weekday Average	Total aged 15+	Social class of head of household		
		ABC1	C2DE	Farming (FIF2)
2000/2001 Universe:	2,963,000	1,111,000	1,496,000	356,000
ANY RADIO REACH	88%	89%	87%	91%
Audience Size 000s	2,610	991	1,296	323
Any RTE Radio 1/2 FM/Lyric FM reach	54%	62%	47%	54%
Audience Size 000s	1,595	692	710	192
RTE Radio 1 Reach	30%	40%	22%	36%
Audience Size 000s	902	441	335	127
2 FM Reach	28%	29%	28%	22%
Audience Size 000s	827	325	424	78
Lyric FM reach	3%	7%	2%	1%
Audience Size 000s	99	72	24	2
Today FM reach	15%	19%	12%	12%
Audience Size 000s	430	206	181	43
Any local station reach	55%	46%	58%	69%
Audience Size 000s	1,635	515	873	247

Source: Joint National Listenership Research Survey, 2000/2001 (MRBI Ltd.) ©

Newspaper readership: national social class data, July 2000 to June 2001

JNRR/Lansdowne Survey, July 2000-June 2001 Average Readership	Total aged 15+	Social class of head of household		
		ABC1	C2DE	Farming
2000/2001 Universe:	2,963,000	1,111,000	1,496,000	356,000
ANY MORNING PAPER	46.5%	57.2%	37.9%	49.1%
Readership 000s	1,403	648	578	178
The Irish Independent	19.8%	27.5%	11.9%	28.6%
Readership 000s	596	311	182	103
The Irish Times	10.1%	22%	3.2%	2.2%
Readership 000s	305	249	48	8
The Star	14.9%	8.6%	21.1%	8.6%
Readership 000s	450	98	322	31
The Irish Examiner	7.7%	8.2%	5.8%	13.8%
Readership 000s	231	93	88	50

Source: Joint National Readership Research Survey, 2000/2001 (Lansdowne Market Research Ltd.) ©

in our own interest: the growth area in terms of audiences for many of us is in working-class areas.

Should newspapers like the *Irish Times* be looking for ways into working-class areas? After all, there is a special student price for that paper, so why not a special price in disadvantaged areas? Why is that notion so outrageous? We constantly hear of promotions, whereby newspapers are given away free: should less well-off areas also be targeted? Is it too much to ask that media empires should also have a social dimension and responsibility?

Looking at the figures again (Table 1), we see that local stations have a much greater and broader penetration in their respective areas than do the national stations, with many having a much higher percentage of the working-class audience. But do people who feel socially excluded, who may have on-air access to local stations, feel they are making a difference in terms of influencing national debate and decision-making?

The dilemma is how to attract working-class audiences. Of course, much of what happens in the media—or indeed middle-class life as expressed through the media—alienates them. But if we set out to attract working-class audiences, this in turn will change the nature of our programmes. Will it in turn change the nature of the working-class audience?

Why don't working-class people go for speech radio with the same energy as their middle-class counterparts? Whose fault is it? Is it a problem? If so, is it a problem that can be fixed? Sure, don't working-class people know what we think is good for them?

If programmes are a complex mix of production, input, feedback, pressures and deadlines, how far can you tweek without weakening your audience? Indeed should we not just push for a media product that simply appeals to the biggest number of people. But, in the eyes of the advertiser, how many working-class people does it take to make one 'professional' consumer?

Is poverty boring?

In truth it is seen to be so by many in the media. Even when it is not boring, is it believable? A few years ago, I happened to arrive along during an eviction and broadcast it live. It had all the ingredients of 'great radio': a ticking clock, a row, a beginning, middle and end, different voices. Yet the onslaught of middle-class angst, disbelief and annoyance generated by that broadcast was terrifying. One newspaper trawled through court records to discover that the woman concerned had got compensation for a fall a few years earlier. This was enough as far as they were concerned to overturn the references of the St Vincent de Paul Society and the local Money Advice Bureau. On the other hand, an eviction last year of two wealthy elderly women by a wealthy relative got widespread newspaper and radio coverage, with nothing but sympathy—rightly—for the old people concerned.

I do not believe there is a middle-class conspiracy in the media to exclude poor people or groups—life is much more complicated than that—just as I do not believe there is an anti-church or anti-family agenda permeating Montrose, Abbey Street or Mid-West Radio.

Part of the onus to make issues around poverty interesting must fall on those groups and individuals who want the media to take an interest in their situation. Poverty, social exclusion and powerlessness can be riveting radio or copy—but too often the 'community and voluntary pillar' expect to get publicity around big set-piece news conferences of whatever—while refusing to bend to the story of an individual, family or group, which is a much better way of getting an audience.

It is worth reminding groups that we all work in a competitive environment—newspapers fight each morning, radio and TV stations vie for audiences—and even within radio stations the competition is intense. Indeed from my own programme's point of view, I regard Marian Finucane and Pat Kenny as bigger competitors than Oprah Winfrey, who is on TV at the same time as *Liveline*.

If these groups wish to get publicity, they have to be prepared to make the same concessions to the media as they make with the Government: in other words, they simply cannot expect programmes and papers to run to their agenda—there has to be give and take. They could simply decide to forget about the media, or they must make a decision as to what, if anything, they want from it.

O Lord, won't you buy me a Mercedes Benz!
The whole push in Irish society is to chase the Celtic Tiger—they are even advertising Mercedes Benz cars on *Liveline*! *Liveline* sees itself as a broad, access-based programme, all for the price of a local call. So why is Mercedes Benz advertising during our one-hour slot? Their ad is a re-run of the Janis Joplin song:

> O Lord, won't you buy me a Mercedes Benz,
> My friends all drive Porsches,
> I must make amends.
> Worked hard all my life,
> With no help from my friends,
> O Lord, won't you buy me a Mercedes Benz!

And this says it all: the economy is so buoyant, so uplifted, so awash, that Mercedes Benz are advertising all over the place. Of course *Liveline* listeners objected to the blasphemy in the ad, the avarice and the quality of the singing. But on a serious note, it made me question the real effects of the so called Celtic Tiger—and the people Mercedes Benz are leaving behind at the bus stops.

Interrogating journalists

As journalists interrogate the powerful and elite in Ireland, it is important that they interrogate their own work, assumptions, attitudes, and language. In Ireland today there has been, thankfully, some exposure by the media of cosy cartels and golden circles—individuals and groups of common economic or political interest. That same energy and questioning should be turned on our own work.

Of course it goes without saying (that's why I'm saying it), that journalists in all the media have contributed enormously over the past few years to a greater understanding of the class nature of Irish society—that the rich look after the rich, and the powerful mind the powerful. This in turn has meant that journalists are now one of the most powerful groups—if not the most powerful—in Irish society. So let's not be afraid to turn our pens, cameras, microphones and minds to a group that is so highly regarded in Ireland: the media.

While recent surveys show that young people have as much interest in politics as Richard Harris has in playing Frank McCourt in 'Angela's Ashes II', the schools of journalism are as overcrowded as a one-room tenement in the Limerick of the 1930s. So journalism is popular. But journalists should be careful not to run away with this new-found power—we don't save lives: if RTE went off the air tomorrow, no one would die. While we do make a difference, we don't save lives! Indeed when RTE staff went on strike a few years ago, nobody died because of it. The contribution of the newspapers is similarly modest.

Recently there has been a disturbing trend for journalists to rely on journalists' views of what other journalists have written or said. For example, in a recent edition of *Prime Time*, RTE's flagship current affairs programme, there was a bizarre scenario of one RTE journalist interviewing an *Irish Times* journalist about the opinions just expressed by a *Sunday Tribune* journalist! And RTE is by no means the biggest offender in the 'journalistic received wisdom' stakes. Prick up your ears when you hear or read one journalist going on about the opinions of another journalist.

More money, more choice

One positive aspect of the upsurge in the economy should be greater choice in the media and greater access for different groups. The success of Lyric FM, RTE's classical music station (especially in the letters page of the *Irish Times*), is a case in point. RTE Radio is launching two new projects on medium wave. One is targeted at the whole area of illiteracy, where the latest figures show that up to 20% of Irish people have difficulties in this area. Radio is a wonderful medium in this regard. The other group addressed is the fifty thousand non-nationals in Ireland: RTE has also launched a special service for them. Could newspapers be equally creative in this area?

We need to interrogate—almost daily—the way the less well-off are excluded from the decision-making process. Recall, for example, the full-page ads in the *Irish Times* inserted by the Docklands Development Authority in an effort to attract high-class investment to the north inner city. They showed abandoned filing cabinets on waste ground, as if this was the fault of local people. It later transpired that the derelict land was owned by CIE (one of the main players in the re-development) and the filing cabinets had been abandoned by the same national transport authority.

Another example was the Government's Luas advisory/action group, which effectively decided to abandon the Luas line to Finglas in favour of the route through Drumcondra and Dublin City University (DCU) because 'the public consultation process found that both the DCU and Drumcondra residents wanted the line to go close to them, but there was little or no response in relation to a possible extension to Finglas.' Anyone who has seen the queues at the Finglas bus terminus in Parnell Street knows that there would be an incredible demand and need for additional public transport to that area. Maybe the people in Finglas were too busy queuing for a bus to engage in the 'public consultation', while the residents of Drumcondra and DCU could drive into the Luas office or email them to get this valuable public utility to run 'close to them'.

Over the years we have tried in radio to give a voice to marginalized groups. There have now been seven live broadcasts from inside Irish prisons on national radio. Now that prisoners are allowed one phone call per day, is it not a matter a time before prisoners start ringing phone-in programmes? Our own access programme—*Liveline*—tries to facilitate a broad range of views—and it proves that as a nation we are very radio literate. Still, it could be better and broader.

The language of exclusion

We should examine our language, especially the use of words like 'we', 'us', 'them', 'society'. These words are used by the media in discussions and articles as terms of inclusion, but rather are heard and read as terms of exclusion, especially by the marginalized in society.

Consider the word 'marginalized': it suggests a small space at the side of a page—yet the number of people who are outside the economic, social, political, and power loop in Irish society would bring that margin into the centre of the page.

Consider the use of language, such as a phrase I heard during one radio discussion: 'Now, Minister, we are better off under the Celtic Tiger.' Listen to journalists when they use the 'we'. It is the 'we' of governance and economic power.

But journalists are not the only offenders—or maybe they are just speaking the truth: that we are an important part of the golden, cosy, smug elite that controls Irish society. Even organisations working for the poor use exclusive language: one radio ad included the phrase 'Thank you for helping them'. Obviously they think poor people are deaf!

And listen carefully to the myriad of middle-class assumptions in the ads. For example, a current ad for endowment policies features a mature female uttering the immortal line 'and we had Orla due for college'. Take it further and ask why the AA *Roadwatch* Dublin accent has now become the voice of choice on the national airwaves. Is it just more melodic, or is it that this is simply how the majority of people in the country now speak?

Demystifying the powerful

The media should try to demystify powerful institutions. However, eulogies often replace critical appraisal, as was seen with some judicial appointments to the Supreme and High Courts. A selection of adjectives for these supermen ranged from 'profoundly dedicated' to 'naturally brilliant', a 'thinker and a scholar', 'one of Ireland's sharpest legal thinkers', with equally glowing references to their 'humanity and integrity'. Running away with themselves, one newspaper actually said that the new Chief Justice had been known to use public transport! Let's thank God that he doesn't live in Finglas, because he'd never be able to travel to the Four Courts on the tram. No wonder people are afraid of the courts! Are we even worthy to live in the same country as those who will judge us?

And yes, we should be serious about our jobs, our role and our responsibilities. But every now and again it is important to remind ourselves that, on any given day, David Trimble, Charlie McCreevy, and Bertie Ahern might be preoccupied with getting their kids tickets to see Mr Potato Head, Buzz Lightyear and Woodie in *Toy Story 2*.

By nature, journalists question. We must spend part of our time questioning ourselves.

Broadcasting and suffering: the Omagh bombing and paramilitary 'punishment beatings'

MICHAEL BEATTIE

In 1977, I was doing one of my first studio interviews for Ulster Television (UTV) and it was my very first studio interview with a large clerical gentleman well known in politics. Just around that time he had savaged a few interviewers, and I must confess that I found myself a little nervous, with quite a few minutes to chat with him before the camera crew was ready to record the interview.

I asked the said clerical gentleman if he felt anyone had ever got the better of him in an interview. He paused for a moment and then said, 'Yes. The first few interviews I ever did, because I answered the questions I was asked.'

Well, I think he and a lot of other politicians are still answering their own questions. I'm no politician, so I intend to deal with the subject of broadcasting and suffering fairly and frankly. First of all, I'll take some time to indicate how I see the background to the job I do, and the kind of pressures I see affecting 'serious programming', if I can call it that: the kind of programmes that deal with suffering, and the kind of programmes that sometimes can be difficult to watch. And then I'll refer specifically to some programmes I've made which give the title to this chapter.

A couple of years ago I discovered an amazing fact: that in 1983 the Tuareg, the largest tribe of nomads in the Sahara, delayed by 10 days their annual migration across the desert, the first time this had happened in thousands of years. And why?—So that they could catch the final episode of 'Dallas'. Don't let anyone underestimate the power of broadcasting!

Around the same time, I came across a piece of text which quite shocked me, and gave me a great deal of food for thought. It is from a book for which I grew to have huge affection.

> A single black cloud with all the war, perversion, violence and crime of the world rolling around inside it. Locked deep in its belly were distant shrieks and the sound of gunfire. Explosive with aboriginal evil, it would travel anywhere—but anywhere—in the land to seek out any

form of violence: an axe attack here, a murder there, a rape, a bomb, a riot—forever pursuing the new and ignoring the same, always turning its back on harmony and fomenting racial strife, ever happy to be a disciple of terror and anxiety while despising the stable and meek. But, more than anything, this cloud of violence loved gorging itself on wars and ignored peace totally. At a moment's notice, this cloud would zoom off to feed on a war in any part of the world. The issues were irrelevant as long as, somewhere, there was strife, death and bullets. Only the face of evil ever attracted the eyes and radar of this cloud.

How about that for a description of the business I've been in for most of my professional life—television news and current affairs? It's a pretty damning description and comes from a former Fleet Street journalist, Tom Davies. Another hack, Paul Johnson, in his Saturday Essay in the *Daily Mail* in October 1999, bluntly described my business as one of the ways in which we barbarise, brutalise and dehumanise the young.

Chris Rea said much the same thing in a song he wrote a couple of years ago, 'Tell me there's a heaven', which became quite popular. He wrote it after his little daughter had been upset by some pretty grim television news footage. If I recall correctly, he wrote another song at that time, directed at the news media, called 'You must be crazy'. Television certainly hasn't sold us short on images of suffering.

In *Media in Ireland: the search for diversity*, RTE's Director-General, Bob Collins, said that 'the responsibility of people in the media is greater than that of people working in many other areas of public life.' And in an article in *Media Report*, Paul Harman wrote that 'it used to be said, the hand that rocks the cradle rules the world—now it seems to be the hand of the television producer.'

I don't want to overestimate the importance and responsibility of the media. But it's one of the main reasons why I make television programmes. And I love making television programmes, serious television programmes. I think they are so important, or they can be, particularly now, at a time when a lot of the broadcast media continue to 'dumb down', with style taking precedence over content, with the cult of the 'television personality', with the desire for high audience figures above all else.

I was quite bemused not so long ago to overhear a reporter from a Belfast newspaper grilling a colleague of mine for gossip about front-of-camera staff in UTV. His boss had a new 'stardust' policy: he wanted his paper to have any snippet of information, preferably negative, about anyone seen on UTV—the journalist as 'star'. The problem is that some of them actually believe it!

The admirable John Cole, former BBC Political Editor and deputy editor of *The Observer*, spoke at a Royal Television Society gathering a couple of years ago about the priority being given to presentation, which was getting in the way of enterprising journalism. His view was that this approach inevitably infects talented young reportérs and correspondents. 'They're not daft', he said, 'they detect which way the prevailing—and promotional—wind is blowing'.

In his article in *Media Report*, Paul Harman was greatly taken with an essay by the Austrian philosopher Karl Popper, in which he referred to meeting the head of a German TV channel who argued that it was his job to provide people with what they wanted, that audience ratings were the best means of judging this, and that it was all, of course, based on the principles of democracy. Popper was aghast. There were no principles to justify this thesis. All it would do is continually lower the quality of programmes.

Of course I examine the ratings. Of course they're important. But if they were the sole basis of judging *Insight's* success, UTV would drop it tomorrow and get twice the audience every Monday night at 10 o'clock by transmitting some comedy series or sit-com bought in at minimal cost from America or Australia.

UTV is first and foremost a commercial organisation. That means the primary responsibility of its senior managers is to the shareholders. Over the past ten years, ratings have become increasingly important to UTV, and UTV has been phenomenally successful in getting them.

To boost the audience figures, a few years back we hired a consultant, a consultant from America, from the most competitive television market in the world, but which also produces surely some of the worst television in the world. Thankfully, Charles Munro, the consultant in question, was a fine man and I learnt a great deal from him. But I have to say that many of us really did cringe when he played us tape after tape from US TV stations, some of them hugely successful, and showed the tricks they used to boost their audience.

Well, whether or not it was down to our 'versioning' of those tricks, it wasn't too long before our teatime news audience was regularly double that of BBC Northern Ireland, peaking at three times as high. Yet, night after night, the BBC were producing an often excellent news programme, with individual reports as good as or better than ours.

Sadly, I now fear that even the dear old BBC in Northern Ireland, the public service broadcaster after all (where I used to work, and for which I retain a great affection), is altering its approach in the hope of catching better ratings. I may be wrong, but I sense a change in series like their 'Home Truths' documentary strand, which for several years has produced first-class films dealing sensitively with some heavy-duty issues.

What did the last series include? One programme was a kind of rock'n'roll hairdressing show, following finalists to the big cut competition. Another showed two middle-aged North Down ladies trying to 'find themselves' in Las Vegas and driving through the Nevada desert, a kind of later life Thelma and

Louise. These were programmes that would have sat much more happily in UTV's much more overtly populist schedule.

I've been making television programmes for more than 20 years. A lot of those programmes—too many of them—have involved people who have suffered. I could adopt a theoretical approach and write at arm's length about suffering as an issue. But I'd prefer to deal with it at a more personal level, with specific reference to two *Insight* programmes which made a particular impact. But allow me to preface that by saying that I don't hold *Insight* up as some kind of paragon: with more than 40 programmes each year, many pass without remark while others generate a lot of criticism.

We're incredibly incestuous in news and current affairs. We're all watching and listening to what the others are doing. We all feed off each other. But I fear that sometimes that blinds us all to the obvious. We're so busy looking at each other that we ignore what's under our noses.

In 1999 I produced a programme on what are euphemistically referred to as 'punishment attacks': paramilitary thugs beating, maiming and abusing their victims, expelling them from their homes and indeed sometimes from the country. In some cases, this was for an alleged misdemeanour in a local community, at worst for no reason other than spite, revenge or settling old scores. This took place while we were supposedly enjoying the benefits of a ceasefire.

Some argue that the media generally knew full well what was going on and deliberately ignored it. They suggested that reporters were sucked into the so-called 'peace process' and didn't want to upset the applecart by highlighting what the hard men associates of some of our newly-democratised politicians were doing.

A week after the programme was transmitted, Henry McDonald wrote in *The Observer*: 'In working-class housing estates across the Province, terror reigns despite the peace process. It's akin to a micro-totalitarianism—and no one gives a damn.' He continued:

> Much of the mainstream media also ignores this micro-totalitarianism. Two weeks ago, the IRA took out their guns and shot a man in the legs in west Belfast. BBC Northern Ireland relegated this story to a few seconds of pictures, with words read by one of their presenters. There was no investigation into who was responsible or into the implications. There are, of course, honourable exceptions. A recent UTV *Insight* into the human cost of republican and loyalist paramilitary beatings was one of the most courageous films since this peace process began. But this investigation stands out particularly because of its singularity; there are lamentably few journalists who are prepared to take on those who have become the paragons of peace and democracy at Stormont.

I'm not sure whether those of us involved in the programme thought of it as courageous. It certainly did make an impact. It made its impact because it showed—in a powerful way—the suffering endured by three people, three among so many. These were:

- Andrew Peden: seven men, possibly more, beat him for ten hours before using a shotgun to blast him in both knees. Why?—Because he took the wrong side in an argument between two of his acquaintances—one in the UDA and one in the UVF—over a woman.

- Jacqueline Burke: savagely beaten and exiled from her home for no reason we could establish.

- Maureen Kearney, who sadly has died since: her son, murdered by the IRA in Belfast, apparently because he had floored the local IRA commander in a fistfight. He was shot in both legs and left to bleed to death. His killers jammed the lift to his flat to stop him getting out or help getting in.

I was deeply affected by what we discovered making that programme and wanted to pass on that sense of horror and outrage to the viewers. No one deserves treatment like the victims we showed. I deliberately set out to shock in the hope that it might encourage others to realise the futility of this kind of violence.

I built up a short opening sequence, the shots showing a couple drinking coffee together: what appeared to be a normal couple in an everyday scene. It could have taken place in a canteen or coffee shop—the focus was on them, not on the background. I used a slight 'slo-mo' effect and some ominous, minor-key instrumental music to create a sombre tone. Then we saw their wedding photograph, then a picture of the husband and his son sitting side-by-side on holiday, wearing their swimming trunks. The screen went black for a moment and, as the music changed to an unearthly female wail, suddenly we saw the husband struggling from his wheelchair onto a hospital bed, with the camera showing both stumps of his amputated legs and his face grimacing with obvious pain.

The opening shot showed Andrew and Linda Peden from the waist up. There was no way of knowing he had no legs. From the family album I deliberately chose the picture of Andrew and his son in their swimming trunks, because their legs were so obvious. That was the last image before we saw Andrew's amputated limbs.

Drinking coffee, a wedding photograph, a holiday photograph. The 'ordinary' things in life that we can all identify with. I wanted viewers to see something of themselves in those scenes and to feel all the more the horror of what happened to Andrew Peden. Apart from the physical horror, I also wanted the audience to feel the rawness of the psychological and emotional damage. From a lengthy interview with Andrew, I used primarily his references to 'ordinary' things we can all identify with, things we take for granted but which he can no longer enjoy. His lips were quivering with emotion and his voice was on the verge of breaking when he described how he could no longer take his daughter to the local café on Saturday mornings. His hurt was equally obvious when he described how his son had thrown himself on the bed crying because his daddy couldn't take him to the 'swimmers' any more.

I can't judge how it might have affected viewers, but I cried my eyes out, time and again, while we made that programme, particularly over the interview with Andrew Peden. I consciously made very heavy use of it because I wanted other people to cry too. I wanted everybody to cry. It was clear that he was in anguish. I talked not only to Andrew and Linda Peden, but to his surgeon and his psychologist. They were both very wary and initially feared that the interview might do him more harm than good; but it was largely because of Andrew's interview, that an ignored story suddenly became prominent. Every national broadsheet took it up, national television too. It even made international news.

Jacqueline Burke, exiled in England, was sadly forgotten after the programme. But, in the way that journalists feed off each other, Andrew Peden and Maureen Kearney were interviewed in story after story. I don't doubt that the impact of that huge coverage was instrumental in forcing the political parties to rein in their hard men at that time.

When I was first being trained as a journalist, I remember being told that we had to be 'all things to all men', that that was the way to get stories. Of course, in television, there are requirements in terms of fairness, impartiality and balance under the Broadcasting Act and, in my case, the Independent Television Commission code, that don't apply to newspapers. But the danger of all that is that programme-makers often emasculate themselves. They balance this and that, interview so many pro's and so many anti's, and project themselves into some kind of detached moral high ground, proclaiming themselves to be 'impartial', whatever that actually means.

Well, I think it's OK to be partial. I think it's OK for programme-makers to be angry and upset, and to admit it. It's OK to weep with those who weep, as well as laugh with those who laugh. And it's OK for television to portray the grief and suffering of individuals, to share in it—gently and sensitively—if those individuals are willing to expose themselves. It's not undignified. In fact, it's the only way to treat victims like this with any kind of dignity.

In making programmes like these, I believe the best thing to do sometimes is to 'feel' what to do, not sit and analyse things out of existence. I've worked in situations in the past which would have involved sitting down with six

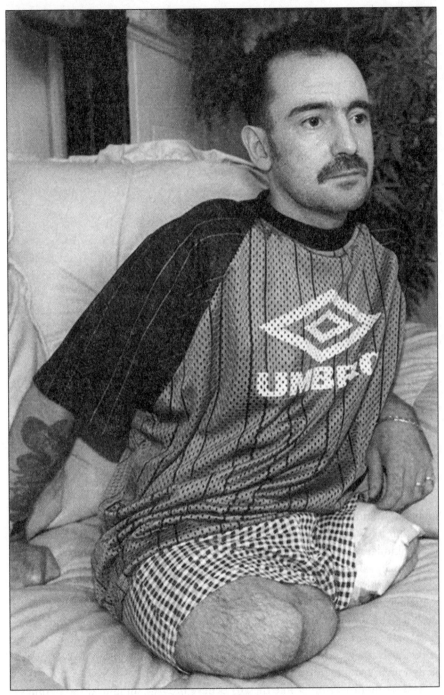

Andrew Peden
Photograph courtesy of Pacemaker Belfast

executives for half-a-day to debate whether it was right to show those brutal pictures of Andrew Peden's legs.

One of the advantages of working in a commercial organisation like UTV is that even to consider that luxury—if indeed that's what it is to have a think-tank of managers—is denied. I usually work with a researcher and a reporter, with a film crew for three days a week, and with a picture editor for three days a week. There isn't much time left to sit and ponder and analyse. If you supposed there were lengthy editorial debates, it's more likely a ten-minute discussion with a colleague, poring over tapes at one o'clock in the morning.

A friend of mine for many years is John Davis, or John T. Davis to give him his full title—probably the country's most acclaimed documentary maker. Now I certainly don't put my very quick-turnaround current affairs programmes in the same league as his carefully crafted films. But it has often amused me to hear academics discussing John's films and giving them layers of rationale and understanding that go way beyond anything John ever meant. There are times when John knows instinctively what's right to do—without a moment's analysis—he 'feels' it.

When you're sitting listening to someone tell you what they've gone through in having their wife, daughter, grand-daughter and unborn grand-daughter blown to pieces, when you go through the tapes again and again into the early hours of the morning with the tears tripping you, you know what to do. You know what they want you to do. And you know they don't want their suffering talked away round a boardroom table. I'm referring to Mick Grimes from Omagh, a quiet, dignified, gentleman, a gentle man, whom we interviewed for an hour-long programme marking 40 days after the Omagh bombing.

I had the same experience when little schoolboy Oran Doherty's sisters in Buncrana described how he used to dance into the living room, pretending to be Michael Flatley. It was almost as if they expected him to come in the next moment, while their father sat shattered in the corner of the room listening, but unable to speak. And Claire Gallagher's mother, a nurse who tended the injured in Omagh hospital and found her daughter, blinded in both eyes, barely recognisable amongst the victims.

They, and other victims, wanted to talk. They hated the way that the 'single black cloud' of media vultures descended on them for a few days and then left for something grim elsewhere. They were trying to make some sense of what had happened. They wanted people to listen to them; they didn't want to be forgotten. I was not putting words on something I sensed from them. It was what they actually said. And if they have something they want to say, do we not have a responsibility to listen?

In the programme on the aftermath of the Omagh bombing, we had some of the first people on the scene describe what happened. It was very graphic, and one of those occasions where we had a five-minute discussion in the cutting

Omagh, 15 August 1998
Photograph courtesy of Pacemaker Belfast

room: how far should we go, will we offend viewers, will we offend relatives of victims who might be hearing this kind of description for the first time?

Once again, in this programme, I was determined not to shy away from the full horror of that awful event. Even after all the news coverage, there remained a huge untold story. I kept thinking of James Simmons's song about the bombing of Claudy—an immensely powerful song that focuses on the very ordinary things of village life, and how these were devastated in a moment. That's what I tried to capture in that television programme.

A number of victims and their relatives—many who hadn't spoken about the event until that point—simply told their story of that dreadful day. We extended the programme to an hour to allow more time for those stories: gracious, gentle people whose lives had been turned upside down.

I also took the decision to use some very graphic and horrific descriptions by people who were close to the site of the bomb. People who saw others die in front of them, who saw limbs and brains lying in the street. I was concerned that we might offend relatives of those who died, but it seemed that the people of Omagh wanted others to know just how they had suffered. Both before and after the programme, I was encouraged to learn that they considered that the right decision had been made.

This was another programme where I wanted the audience to weep with those who were weeping and I'm not ashamed of that. The final sequence included a memorial service held in the local High School, where five of the victims had been pupils or former pupils. In the closing sequence we showed individual photographs of all the victims and, looking at those faces, young and old, I knew it would have the desired effect. I hoped that somewhere, in the midst of those tears, even one hard heart had been softened.

People are quick to complain about television programmes, but not so quick to respond positively. The Omagh programme generated quite a lot of calls and letters, and only one of them was negative. For me, there were two important reactions. Firstly, from a number of normally cynical fellow journalists. But, more importantly, from the people who were there. One of the most pleasing responses for me was from an Omagh person who wrote:

> The programme had the pace and style of a country wake ... it was perfectly pitched ... I am confident that it will help in the grieving of the afflicted in Omagh, Buncrana and further afield.

It's more than twenty years since Lady Mountbatten suffered the heartache of losing her son, her father, her mother-in-law and a young family friend from Enniskillen in one bomb blast. For weeks she lay in pain, heartbroken and in agony. My friend, the columnist Alf McCreary, met her some time later and was thoroughly impressed with her gentleness and compassion.

She told him that she had learnt—and we can all learn—from suffering. She said: 'I believe my experience of suffering has sharpened my sense as to what other people have to go through.' Her advice to the bereaved was to talk, not to bottle their feelings in. Her advice to the rest of us was: if we knew a person who had lost someone near and dear, particularly in tragic circumstances, to do something to show that we care. 'It's much easier to bear if you feel you're not alone,' she said.

The kind of programmes I've referred to have the potential to do all sorts of things on different levels. They can help victims feel they're not alone: they know that many, many people are weeping with them.

And, although as producers and viewers we are one step removed, I feel that programmes like these can help us learn a little more—sharpen our senses, as Lady Mountbatten said—about the nature of suffering and the nature of a society where horrible, tragic events like this can happen.

The media, propaganda and the Northern Ireland peace process

DAVID MILLER

The situation in relation to freedom of expression in Northern Ireland has improved markedly as a result of the peace process. The most obvious sign of this is the lifting of the broadcasting ban on Sinn Féin and ten other organisations after the first IRA ceasefire in 1994. But there have been marked improvements elsewhere as well. One of the key limits on the freedom of expression of the British media (and in particular television) was the successful use of intimidation by successive Governments to prevent the airing of views critical of British policy in Ireland. There is a long history of such pressures which noticeably intensified in the 1980s (see Curtis, 1998; Miller, 1994, chapter 2). Following the ceasefires and the lifting of the Government broadcasting ban, the atmosphere in television, which had become freer with the peace process, moved a further step. In particular, interviews with members of the IRA were broadcast on British television for the first time since 1974 (in a programme by Ros Franey, 'Talking to the enemy': see Miller, 1995a & 1995b).

It was also noticeable that interviews with republicans became less hostile as the peace process advanced, which showed the broadcasters making at least minimal editorial changes to reflect the central role of Sinn Féin in the peace process (Lago, 1998; Miller, 1995b & 1997).

Given the changed orientations of British Government policy and the prospect of peace, there was little appetite for intimidating the media and in a way it suited the British Government that Sinn Féin should come in from the cold as part of the peace process. Furthermore, the broadcasters showed little desire to engage in previous levels of current affairs and documentary coverage. The deregulation of television has resulted in tighter budgets and less space for investigative journalism and current affairs in general. And the end of the 'war' in Northern Ireland has encouraged previously secretive activists (republicans and loyalists as well as British operatives) to start to tell their stories.

This chapter looks at developments in the coverage of the peace process and at the way in which the British Government especially has handled its information function. It begins with an account of the intensified pressures on the media in relation to secrecy and anti-terrorism legislation and moves on to examine the Northern Ireland Information Service (NIIS) and its activities.

Next it gives an account of media coverage and editorial priorities in the peace process. Finally, it raises questions about how the media and Government information services need to be reformed as part of the peace settlement.

Secrecy and anti-terrorism legislation
Despite the lack of intimidation of the media, the use of secrecy and anti-terrorism legislation against the media has intensified. There have been a fairly large number of books published since the peace process which have revealed varying details about the 'secret' or 'dirty' war in Northern Ireland. But it has been mainly those books which attempt to reveal information about abuses of the law by the intelligence services, the army and police which have found themselves on the end of court orders or attempts at suppression.

There are two important exceptions to this, both of which relate to the IRA. The killing of Eamon Collins (1997) and the shooting of Martin McGartland (1998) by republicans (if not by the IRA) may be seen as being connected with the books both men had written (and in the case of Collins, the statements they had made to the media and elsewhere). Even if these men were not targeted solely for their public statements and accounts, this was certainly related to the attacks on them.

The British Government has not generally attempted to interfere with the accounts of the activities of British informers in the republican movement (see such books as: Collins, 1997; Gilmour, 1999; McGartland, 1998 & 1999; O'Callaghan, 1999) or with accounts from former agents which have been vetted by the Ministry of Defence (such as Lewis, 1999). Instead there have been a string of cases recently which raise profound questions about freedom of expression and in particular the ability of Northern Ireland to move on and put the past behind it in a full and frank acknowledgement of the crimes of all sides in the conflict. These cases include:

- the arrest of author Tony Geraghty and one of his alleged sources in relation to his book on the troubles and the reluctance of his publisher to issue the paperback version (see Geraghty, 2000a).
- the attempt to interfere with the book written by Jack Holland (Holland and Phoenix, 1997) about the life of one of the RUC intelligence operatives killed on the Mull of Kintyre.
- the court order made against Ed Moloney (Northern Editor of the *Sunday Tribune*) in an attempt to force him to divulge his sources on collusion between the 'security services' and loyalist paramilitaries.
- the Saville inquiry's attempt to force British journalists to reveal details of sources.
- the gagging order imposed on the *Sunday Times* following its revelations about illegal burglary and arson of the Stevens inquiry premises by the

army's secret intelligence unit, the Force Research Unit (see Clarke, 1999; *Sunday Times*, 1999).

- the arrest of a person alleged to be one of Clarke's sources under the Official Secrets Act. His house was burgled and a book manuscript taken. 'The manuscript turned up a few days later in the hands of the prosecution … when Government lawyers obtained an injunction preventing him from publishing the book' (Norton-Taylor, 2000).
- the subsequent pursuit and arrest of Liam Clarke for writing the stories (see Mullin, 2000)
- the recall and suppression of *She Who Dared*, an account by women intelligence operatives of the highly secretive 14th Intelligence Company,. This occurred 'two months after the ministry itself had "cleared" (i.e. censored) the work' (Geraghty, 2000b).

All of these cases have arisen (to a greater or lesser degree) as a result of the unravelling of the Irish conflict. They have affected the full range of media—press and television as well as publishing. This is quite different to the period of heightened intimidation of broadcasters ushered in by the Thatcher Government. These cases are worrying in that there has been an increase in the resort to legal action to suppress journalistic inquiries and also because they indicate that the British State shows little willingness to acknowledge openly its own role in the 'dirty' war in Northern Ireland. The sheer number of cases relating specifically to Northern Ireland shows the increased willingness of former intelligence and security personnel to begin to variously tell 'their side' of the story and to unburden themselves of some of the more dubious activities of the British State's dirty war. But it also shows the absolute determination of the Ministry of Defence and the security apparatus to conceal past (and present) wrong-doing, from Bloody Sunday, through the policy of selective assassination known as 'shoot-to-kill', to collusion with loyalist paramilitaries. This bodes ill for the peace process and highlights the urgent need for some form of truth-and-reconciliation forum.

Furthermore, legislative developments in the area do not suggest a lessening of attempts by the state to control information about the activities of its agents. In particular, the fact that anti-terrorist legislation has not been and shows no sign of being repealed is worrying. Moreover, recent developments in relation to anti-terrorism legislation, freedom of information legislation and the proposed Bill on the Regulation of Interception and Communication indicate that the British Government is tightening the legislative controls on journalism in relation to Ireland as well as in relation to 'British' politics.

The resources and cultural power of the Northern Ireland Office (NIO) Information Division vastly outstrip those of the political parties in Northern Ireland. There are concerns about how this power is used. For example, the strategy of the Northern Ireland Office (NIO) for 'selling' the Good Friday Agreement, which was leaked to the Democratic Unionist Party, shows an extensive investment in opinion polling by the Government and a highly selective approach to the release of that information. In addition, there remain worries about religious and gender imbalances in the staffing of the Information Service.

Information Service activities
The Northern Ireland Information Service (NIIS) at Stormont has a relatively good reputation for accuracy among journalists. Nevertheless, as the emergence of the peace process has shown, it is certainly more than capable of deliberately misleading journalists and the public. One has only to refer to the debacle over the secret talks with the IRA in 1993 when the Director of Information at the NIO, Andy Wood, scoffed that reports of the talks belonged 'more properly in the fantasy of spy thrillers than in real life' (McKittrick, 1993). But truth in Northern Ireland is stranger than fiction, and the story was confirmed by Sinn Féin on 15 November 1993 and shortly thereafter by the Government itself. The NIIS continues to use the full range of political PR techniques including misleading journalists and massaging information. To the best of my knowledge the NIO itself does not engage in black propaganda, although there remain a lot of spooks about on the Northern Ireland scene who are partial to the occasional bit of fabrication derived from variously reliable and less reliable intelligence reports. The best known of these during the peace process was the incident which alleged a sexual relationship between Sinn Féin's Gerry Kelly and one of Senator George Mitchell's staff. The NIO did not come out of that with a completely blot-free copybook. Rather than killing the story, the NIO, whether intentionally or not, gave it legs by issuing a half-hearted holding statement saying that 'who members of Mr Mitchell's staff met was a matter for the senator and not the NIO' (cited in O'Toole, 1997). This was seen by US Government sources and by a number of journalists as giving 'a nod and a wink' that there was some substance to the story, which there was not.

But peace has demanded a suspension of some of the wilder antics of the spooks. There is no more lying about killings as in the Gibraltar or Stalker 'shoot to kill' cases (although the case of Diarmuid O'Neill, shot by the Metropolitan Police in London in September 1996, is worrying). This is partly because the State has stopped killing people in special-forces' ambushes. Incidentally, did anyone notice that these killings stopped shortly after the British Government started the secret talks with the republican movement in the early 1990s?

This is not to say that the British Government, and in particular the Ministry of Defence and the intelligence agencies, no longer pump out misinformation.

They clearly do and much of it seems designed to undermine the peace process. This suggests that there are interests in the British State—even now—who are trying to undermine the prospect of a lasting peace deal. It is possible that on occasions such stories come from pro-unionist sources in the NIO or the Government. However, the use of British newspapers to plant stories with 'not a scintilla of truth' (in the words of Dr Martin Mansergh, special adviser to the taoiseach, cited in Cullen, 2000, in his report on the Eighth Cleraun Media Conference) does suggest the involvement of the Army, Ministry of Defence and/or MI5.

Instead, we have a much greater role for the full range of modern spin techniques. Many of these are also practised by other British Government departments and increasingly (as Seán Duignan makes clear in his book (1995) and in his address to the Seventh Cleraun Media Conference which is reproduced in Kiberd (1999)), though not to nearly the same extent, by the Irish Government.

Take the example of the referendum over the Good Friday Agreement. Northern Ireland Office (NIO) sources stated that they were neutral in the referendum. The campaign advertising produced by the NIO included the strapline 'It's *Your* Decision'. The Information Service line was:

> This is what has been hammered out by your politicians around the table. This is their view of the way forward. This represents their best attempt to arrive at Government for the foreseeable future of Northern Ireland which is based on consensus and inclusion. It is really down to the people to make up their minds. (Interview with Colin Ross, NIIS, cited in Kirby, 1999: 39)

And yet, in a leaked memo, a different picture emerged of their actual strategy. As the Director of Communications, Tom Kelly, wrote:

> We are embarking on what will be the most crucial election campaign in Northern Ireland's history. During the next ten weeks we need to convince the Northern Ireland public both of the importance of what is at stake, and also convince them that not only is agreement possible, but they have a vital role to play in endorsing it.

One key way in which the NIO tried to boost the campaign was by means of focus and opinion research:

> A key requirement in developing our communications strategy will be a continuing flow of information about public attitudes and response. On some occasions this will be helpful to our cause and on others not so. It will be important therefore to ensure that not all of the results of opin-

ion polling, etc., will be in the public domain.

It would be open to us to encourage some degree of public opinion polling by, for example, newspapers and current affairs programmes, where we believe the results are likely to be supportive. Some of this can be encouraged during meetings and briefings of senior media people. (Kelly, 1998)

These opinion polls are still not in the public domain and Tom Kelly has refused to release them as recently as January 2000. A second example utilises a long-standing technique with a pedigree of at least thirty years—that of encouraging third-party endorsements:

We should, where possible, be enlisting the help of those people to champion our cause, e.g., Robin Eames and other church leaders, the heads of community organisations and trade unions, and other members of the G7. While any overt manipulation could be counterproductive, a carefully co-ordinated timetable of statements from these people will be helpful in giving our message credibility with those they represent. It has the added benefit of providing a fresh face for that message, and ensuring that it is not only Government which is seen to be selling the process.

While information service can do our part, it is essential that other divisions and departments use all their available contacts not only to identify suitable people, but also advise on how best to cultivate their support. Tony McCusker's office is co-ordinating a database of key movers and shakers from all sections of the community. (Kelly, 1998)

We can also note the use of the photograph on the front cover of the agreement booklet sent to every home in Northern Ireland. It showed a family on a beach bathed in a brilliant sunset. Some enterprising photographer noticed that Northern Ireland doesn't have any beaches where such a scene might have been shot and it was eventually acknowledged that the photo was taken in South Africa.

The 1997 internal review of the Northern Ireland Information Service reads very like the similar reviews carried out since Labour came to power: more co-ordination, 24-hour operation, increased strategic thinking, extensive trailing and rapid-rebuttal (NIO, 1997). However, one point to note in the current context of suspicion about the direction of British policy[1] is the way in which David Trimble has tried to use the Information Service in the cause of a

---

1 As Gerry Adams put it, 'Spin-doctoring for Glengall Street (Ulster Unionist HQ) is not in Peter Mandelson's remit': '"Disgraceful Mandelson Undermined Me" Says Adams', PA, 4 February 2000.

kind of Blairite presidentialism. According to sources in the Northern Ireland Office:

> When Trimble first came in, before the rest of the offices were set up, he seems to have had Government press officers writing political speeches for him and doing press releases, and that sort of set a precedent and when the other [UUP] guys came in they were looking to do the same. (Interview with the author, February 2000)

This does suggest that there may be problems ahead for the Executive, and arguments about who the Information Service is there to serve.

Patterns of employment at the NIO
Religious affiliation remains an issue in employment patterns in the Northern Ireland Civil Service. A Fair Employment Agency report concluded in 1983 that the numbers and proportions of Catholics at senior level are 'very small' (p. 13). There have been a number of controversies about religious imbalances in the Civil Service. The most recent Equal Opportunities figures reportedly show that 'Protestants still occupy four times more senior Civil Service posts than Catholics in Northern Ireland' (*Belfast Telegraph*, 2000). It is clear that the recruitment pattern parallels the mindset of many NIO officials. On occasion, this can be expressed openly in what are thought to be secure conditions. Liz Drummond was Chief Press Officer at the Northern Ireland Office in London in 1982–3. She later became Director of Information at the Scottish Office, serving until the arrival of the Labour Government in 1997. She reports her first meeting with a senior member of the press office, Billy Millar, now retired. Over lunch in Belfast the conversation turned to football:

> I told him my father was a professional footballer and he said 'Oh, who did he play for?' and I said 'Scotland and Glasgow Rangers', which of course meant that I was perfectly alright—I was a bluenose. He then took me back to Stormont to look at the press office and as we were approaching it he turned to me and said 'Of course, we've got two of them working here.' I said 'Two of what, Billy?', and he said 'Catholics!' and he said it with such venom I was shocked—I was appalled. I had never seen such blind prejudice. I could not believe that this man in a senior position in a responsible Civil Service job could hold that kind of view. I was a Protestant, I was a patriot, but I was so appalled … That was a bad start, and I just hated it. There were just so many little incidents of bigotry, prejudice, ignorance, I thought I want out of it. (Interview with the author, February 1998, cited in Miller, 1998)

She lasted a year in the NIO. In the first year of the new Labour administration, three Catholics were appointed to Senior Information Officer posts. Meanwhile Andy Wood, the English-born Director of Information, was replaced by Tom Kelly, a northern Protestant. Kelly had been a former news editor at the BBC in Belfast where he was involved in a long-running dispute. According to newspaper reports, the BBC Northern Ireland NUJ chapel unanimously passed a resolution condemning Kelly's behaviour in December 1994. Five employees pursued a formal collective complaint against him, backed by the union. The BBC head of programmes did not uphold the complaint but acknowledged that employees' concerns 'highlighted problems relating to management structures and the need for proper staff appraisal' (see Walker, 1995; *Belfast Telegraph*, 1995).

By mid-1998 the proportion of Catholics at senior positions remained low, with a third of Senior Information Officers being Catholic and only one amongst the most senior eleven posts (Principal Information Officer and above). By February 2000 a new wave of promotion boards had increased the Catholics in the NIIS to three among the top eleven posts (one of whom is English), which is still an under-representation. The Information Service is required to advertise all vacancies in the press. The appointment of the Executive led to the formation of an Executive Information Service which was due to become formally separate from the NIO at the end of March 2000 (but the Executive was suspended before it happened). Each minister in the Executive has a number of press officers. In fact, almost all of the staff serving the nationalist parties were Protestant. I am not suggesting that this was either deliberate or sinister, but it is noteworthy that, according to my information, neither the Social and Democratic Labour Party (SDLP) nor Sinn Féin raised the issue of the religious composition of either their press office or Civil Service staff while the Executive was in operation up to February 2000. Also, the internal management review of the Information Service conducted in late 1997 contains nothing whatsoever about the 'representativeness' of press office staff or about how the Information Service might reshape itself in the new political environment (NIO, 1997). After the Executive was suspended in February 2000, the SDLP did raise the issue of the continued religious imbalance in the Civil Service as a whole (see *Belfast Telegraph*, 2000).

Furthermore, it is also apparent that the Information Service had to confront issues relating to gender. Indeed, one serving member of the service has written publicly about the matter. Maggie Stanfield is the editor of the NIO's glossy magazine *Omnibus*. Writing in *Fortnight*, she noted the experience of working in the Information Service under its former head, Andy Wood:

> The day after I joined the Northern Ireland Office in 1989, my new boss cadged a lift from me. He loathed driving and would do anything

to avoid it. As he got into the car, I moved Roger Hargreaves' 'Mr. Happy' and a four-inch long Ferrari Testarossa off the seat. 'Got a youngster, have you?' It might have been an entirely innocent enquiry, but it sounded faintly accusing. 'Er, yes, just the one,' I responded apologetically. 'You're not married, are you?' I began to feel angry and embarrassed in roughly equal proportions. (Stanfield, 1999)

She decided to study the proportion of women in senior positions in the entire Civil Service:

> By the time I arrived at the NIO, I knew that there was a certain pre-disposition about women on the front line. There were some 20 press officers employed at my grade and the grade above. There were no women at the upper grade and just four of us on the lower one ... More than half the people who joined the NICS (Northern Ireland Civil Service) in 1997 were women (56% of the 650 appointments to the general service grades), yet only 13.6% of those at Grade 7 and above are women. Dr Henrietta Campbell, the Chief Medical Officer, obviously a specialist, is the most senior female civil servant in Northern Ireland. At Assistant Secretary and above, women make up just 9.3%. When it comes to the Big-Money Posts advertised by the Civil Service Commission; heads of agencies like construction or engineering; head of something like the IDB (Industrial Development Board) or the Housing Executive; head of the Northern Ireland Information Service: of the 20 appointments made last year, not one was a woman. We have yet to see a female Permanent Secretary or Head of the NI Civil Service.[2]

In Stanfield's view, gender under-representation is a consequence of deep-rooted attitudes:

> The problem is not in the structures. The problem is in the internalised attitudes of men bred upon the Ulster theology: women exist to service the needs of their men-folk. If they insist on trying to compete against men in the job market, then they must accept that they start at a congenital disadvantage. Men do not cast themselves as knights in shining armour out to improve the lot of women. They are conspicuously unchauvinistic at that level. What men are doing is sustaining the disadvantage.

2 The first woman Permanent Secretary has now been appointed.

The issue of continued imbalance in the religious makeup of the Information Service and the Civil Service as a whole clearly needs acknowledgement and remedy for there to be a just and lasting peace. If 'Northern Ireland' is to move away from the 'big boys' rules' of the past, there is also a serious need to tackle gender imbalance in the Civil Service.

Self-censorship and media bias
Concerns about media self-censorship have subsided somewhat since the lifting of the broadcasting ban and the decline of Government intimidation. Furthermore, the broadcasting institutions in Northern Ireland and in Britain have reoriented their coverage of Northern Ireland as a result of the progress of the peace process. In particular, there has been a less hostile approach to interviewing Sinn Féin (Lago, 1998). However, the broadcasting institutions still find it difficult to deal with republican representatives and views. In particular, there has been very little public debate or evidence of internal debate on how the broadcasters might facilitate peace by changing both their reporting guidelines and practice and their recruitment procedures.

There is evidence that British television reporting has been overly reliant on Governmental statements and briefings in the peace process (Miller and McLaughlin, 1996). Television journalists found it exceptionally hard to acknowledge that they had been misled by the Government over the denial of secret talks with the republicans in 1993. Even after Sir Patrick Mayhew acknowledged the contacts, TV news continued to report Government statements as truthful. For example, the BBC reported that while some of the oral messages exchanged 'may be open to question ... we must accept the Government version' (*Newsnight*, 29 November 1993). In fact, the Government version was false and they were forced to change crucial passages in their own documentation to correct 'typographical errors'. As even the *Sunday Telegraph* acknowledged: 'Perhaps the strangest consequence of the process has been that the IRA have now become more believable than the Government' (5 December 1993).

Even then, the Government still maintained a high level of credibility for TV news, and official briefings continued to structure news bulletins. One example is Sinn Féin's request for clarification of the Downing Street declaration. For five months, Ministers repeatedly refused clarification. When they eventually gave it, they referred to "commentary", "elucidation" or "explanation", and British officials tried to play down the response by suggesting that only one of Sinn Féin's questions warranted explanation. BBC news dutifully played along with this line, reporting 'the Northern Ireland Secretary had clarified one point only' (2100 19 May 1994). In fact the Government response ran to 21 pages and included several new departures.

In addition the BBC has come under some criticism for its reporting of the

Orange Order disturbances at Drumcree and elsewhere. In particular, there is a tendency to treat Orange parades as matters of either cultural expression or as the focus of disputes, rather than as expressions of dominance. The key problem is that the view of Orangeism as fundamentally sectarian is extremely rarely reported and explained—far less endorsed—by British broadcasters, while the other views are.

This is especially clear during the marching season in the three-way confrontations between local nationalists, the Orange Order and the RUC. The examples below are from coverage of the marches in 1995.

Television news showed a tendency to contextualise the demonstrations as quaint, somehow absurd traditions to which there could be no serious objection, except, perhaps, from people with strong (nationalist) political views. Thus the BBC endorsed the Orange argument by reporting that they were 'insisting on their right to march a traditional route' (BBC1 2100 10 July 1995). However, as David Sharrock of the *Guardian* put it: 'It is no longer enough to assert that a march should pass through a certain area simply because it has done so for the last 188 years and disregard the views of a local population which has changed radically over that period' (12 July 1995).

ITN were anxious to point out that the 'Orangemen' on the Ormeau Road were 'marching with their wives and families' (ITN 2200 12 July 1995). In such a scenario, it is very difficult to understand why ordinary nationalists might object to, or be afraid of, a carnival-like family procession passing through their streets. ITN made no mention of the sectarian killing of five Catholics at an Ormeau Road betting shop which have made the Orange marches there so sensitive.

As Pamela Clayton shows in her meticulous *Enemies and Passing Friends: Settler ideologies in twentieth century Ulster* (1996), the 'settler' ideologies of Ulster Loyalism, suffused with sectarianism and even racism, have altered little in the course of the twentieth century. Yet such perspectives continue to be marginalised by television news. The closest the BBC got was a reference to the potential of Orange marches to turn into a 'symbol of dominance' (10 July 1995).

The impulse to explain Orange demonstrations as 'tradition' contrasts with a reticence to describe nationalist objections in a similar way. However, when it comes to a clash between the Orange Order and the RUC, there is little contest. Apart from minority news programmes, television news journalists are with the police. An extraordinary example of this occurred during the Portadown stand-off in the run up to the 12th of July parades. As the police and demonstrators squared up to one another for a second night, the RUC fired plastic bullets at the crowd. At the scene, the BBC's reporter opined that the confrontation must be serious because 'the RUC fire plastic bullets only when things are getting quite serious' (BBC1 2100 10 July 1995). Such a view is consistent with the view of the RUC press office but scarcely tells the entire story. Plastic and rubber bullets fired by the police and army have killed 16 people in the past 30 years. In many of these cases, eyewitness accounts suggest either that no confrontation existed or that the victim was not involved (Curtis, 1982).

On the twelfth of July itself, *Channel Four News*, alone on British TV, reported the RUC as arriving on the Ormeau Road at 6am and 'beating residents into the side streets then sealing them off. Several people said they were injured by policemen ... at least four went to hospital.' In stark contrast, both BBC and ITN reports blamed nationalists for outbreaks of violence and neglected to report the RUC violence. The BBC said that 'bottles were thrown' by Catholics but that 'generally the day passed off peacefully' (2100 12 July 1995). Meanwhile, ITN had the police 'trying to keep the sides apart' (1740 12 July 1995).

Such problems with reporting have not gone away in the past five years. In 1998, the *Irish News* published an impassioned front page editorial criticising the BBC coverage of the issue, together with complaints when the BBC broadcast the Orange Order marches live on the twelfth of July (see 'Our leaders have failed us', *Irish News*, 9 July 1998; Liz Trainor and Seamus McKinney, 'Fury over parades coverage by BBC', *Irish News*, 14 July 1998. The BBC justified the broadcast, arguing that 'there is considerable interest in Northern Ireland in live coverage of this event as demonstrated by the high audience figures each year'. This does show a remarkable lack of understanding about the impact of the marches on Catholics in Northern Ireland, and very little rethinking in the BBC on how editorial policy might change with the peace process.

There has been an extensive debate in Northern Ireland about the reforms needed to make the RUC acceptable to all of the community. Yet, strangely, there has been no similar debate about how the BBC and other broadcasters need to change. Is it necessary for the BBC, for example, to change its name to become the Northern Ireland Broadcasting Corporation? Certainly there is a need for the BBC, UTV, ITN and other broadcasters to take stock of how their reporting may be damaging the movement towards peace by acting as if they were still in a war situation. During the war, broadcasters stated unambiguously that they were on the side of the State. But now, in the new circumstances of peace, there has been no repudiation of such institutionalised bias. As a result, some editorial judgements reveal a reflex hostility towards Irish nationalism and republicanism. Thus the complaint by Coiste na n-Iarchimí about the refusal of BBC Northern Ireland to broadcast interviews with their members who are former prisoners. Despite their being released under the Good Friday Agreement and being interviewed as part of the launch of Coiste na n-Iarchimí (which aims to reintegrate republican ex-prisoners), the interviews were pulled. The BBC argued that since one of the interviewees had been convicted of murder and the BBC had no time to contact the family of the victim, the interview could not be shown. The BBC cited a section of their producers' guidelines on interviewing criminals as authority for this, thus neglecting the differences recognised in the Good Friday Agreement between ordinary criminals and political prisoners (see Ritchie, 2000).

Furthermore, the BBC has not taken similar precautions when it has interviewed British Army 'criminals'. For example, the BBC did interview Private Lee Clegg (a British soldier convicted of the murder of an Irish civilian) on his release from prison. The interview was broadcast on the BBC network news (2100 27 February 1998) and on the regional news in the northeast of England (*Look North*, early evening, 27 February 1998). My understanding is that the BBC did not specifically contact the family of Clegg's victim, Karen Reilly, to let them know about this. The BBC in Northern Ireland have stated (letter to the author from Andrew Coleman, Head of News and Current Affairs, 13 September 1999) that Clegg was not interviewed on BBC Northern Ireland and that 'it was, in any event, our practice to contact the relatives of Karen Reilly to seek their reaction to developments in the case'. But contacting the family to comment on the case is quite different to contacting the family to warn them of the interview. It does seem that there is the potential for a double standard operating here.

What should happen next?

The road ahead is not going to be an easy one, but a useful starting point is the report of the UN Special Rapportéur, Abid Hussain (2000), on freedom of expression. His report, which seems not to have been noticed by many in the British or Irish media, makes sweeping recommendations about reforming current legislation and practice. The report breaks new ground in calling for the repeal of emergency legislation on the grounds that it infringes freedom of expression. Also, for the first time, it calls for broadcasters to improve their coverage of Northern Ireland. In a wide-ranging report, the Special Rapporteur calls for the:

- repeal of all emergency laws not in accordance with international treaties and 'in particular ... the Prevention of Terrorism Act which has a chilling effect' on freedom of expression and opinion
- reform of the Official Secrets Act to allow a public interest defence
- narrowing of the scope of the Regulation of Interception and Communication Bill
- review of the Freedom of Information Bill to limit the scope of class exemptions and enhance the powers of the Information Commissioner.

The report calls for the Government to 'disclose information to the victims of the conflict ... to a maximum extent', including publishing the Stalker/Sampson and Stevens inquiries on 'shoot-to-kill' and security force collusion. The report notes the strong reasons for setting up a South African-style Truth and Reconciliation Commission (as suggested by others, including Rolston, 1996). We noted above the apparent campaign by the Ministry of Defence to obscure its misdeeds in the conflict. It is difficult to think of any other means by which such information can be brought to light other than by a formal inquiry or commission with full powers of disclosure.

If Northern Ireland is to move to an open and inclusive system of Government, and if peace is to be entrenched, there will be a need to reform the information function of the NIO. In particular, there needs to be an open and free debate on the extent to which Whitehall spin is justifiable, especially in the context of a fragile peace, and there needs to be serious reform of the staffing of the NIIS to deal with sectarianism and gender imbalance.

In an unusual move, the UN Special Rapporteur criticised the BBC and other broadcasters for their reporting of the peace process: 'Further efforts should be made to improve the media tone and attitude towards Northern Ireland ... the BBC and other broadcasters [should] re-evaluate their guidelines'. The report cites the refusal of the BBC to broadcast interviews it conducted with members of the republican ex-prisoners group discussed above. The BBC's reliance on its guidelines on interviews with criminals as a justification was dismissed by the UN Special Rapporteur as 'creating a confusion between political prisoners and ordinary criminals'.

The BBC, and for that matter UTV, should be considering ways in which they can make sure that sectarian imbalances in staffing are corrected. Such rethinking should also include finding ways to contribute to the reintegration into public life of the participants in the conflict, including ex-prisoners. Furthermore, the broadcasters should take steps to ensure that ex-combatants and former prisoners are not discriminated against in applying for jobs in media organisations.

There is some evidence that some minor changes have occurred at the BBC, but not at UTV or the Independent Television Commission. These can be found in the most recent versions of their producers' guidelines and in the BBC report, *The Changing UK* (1999). Here, for the first time, the BBC notes that 'while interviewees may refer to Northern Ireland as Ulster, our journalists should not use Ulster as a synonym. (Ulster is one of the four provinces of Ireland. It consists of nine counties—the six in Northern Ireland and three in the Republic of Ireland)' (BBC, 1998, chapter 19). Previously, the 1993 *Style Guide* had allowed the use of the term: 'It is acceptable to call it "Ulster" (though not in the first instance) but never "the six counties"' (BBC 1993). A further shift in emphasis is the move from saying that people in Northern Ireland are 'entitled'

(BBC, 1993) to regard themselves as British to a more neutral description: that while some people 'regard themselves as British others regard themselves as Irish' (BBC, 1999: 14). Overall, this is a shift of emphasis which is very much in line with Government thinking on the topic, treating both 'sides' equally and neglecting the role of Britain in the conflict.

But there has been no acknowledgement of past errors, nor have the guidelines governing coverage changed adequately to reflect the peace process. In addition, the BBC's structural unionism (it is the British Broadcasting Corporation) also hampers the development of adequate news coverage.

Finally, there is a need for openness and debate on the future. Otherwise no serious reform will occur, and the profoundly undemocratic politics and decision-making of the past thirty years may well transfer themselves to the new institutions.

References

BBC (1993) *Style Guide*, London: BBC. Reprinted in B. Rolston, and D. Miller (ed.) (1996) *War and Words: The Northern Ireland Media Reader*, Belfast: Beyond the Pale.
BBC (1998) *Producers Guidelines*, London: BBC. www.bbc.co.uk/info/editorial/prodgl.shtml
BBC (1999) *The Changing UK*, March, London: BBC.
Belfast Telegraph (1995) '"Staff unhappy" as BBC clears editor', 15 May.
Belfast Telegraph (2000) 'Bias in Civil Service continues, claims SDLP' 15 April.
Carvajal, D. (1999) 'Northern Ireland Book's Allegations Stir International Libel Fight', *New York Times*, 9 August. www.nytimes.com/library/tech/99/08/biztech/articles/09libel.html
Clarke, L. (1999) 'Secret army unit burnt police files', *Sunday Times*, 21 November.
Clayton, P. (1996) *Enemies and Passing Friends: Settler ideologies in twentieth century Ulster*, London: Pluto.
Collins, E. with McGovern, M. (1997) *Killing Rage*, London: Granta Books.
Cullen, P. (2000) 'Taoiseach's adviser urges media to give more "space" to peace negotiators', *Irish Times*, 14 February.
Curtis, L. (1982) *They Shoot Children: The use of rubber and plastic bullets in the North of Ireland*, London: Information on Ireland.
Curtis, L. (1998) *Ireland: the Propaganda War*, updated edition, Belfast: Sásta.
Duignan, S. (1995) *One Spin on the Merry-Go-Round*, Dublin: Blackwater Press.
Geraghty, T. (2000a) 'Whitehall's war on me', *The Guardian*, Media, 7 February: 10.
Geraghty, T. (2000b) 'She said too much', *The Guardian*, 26 February: 22.
Gilmour, R. (1999) *Dead Ground: Infiltrating the IRA*, London: Warner.
Holland, J. and Phoenix, S. (1997) *Phoenix: Policing the Shadows*, London: Coronet.
Hussain, A. (2000) *Civil and Political Rights, including the Question of Freedom of Expression*, Report submitted by Mr Abid Hussain, Special Rapporteur, in accordance with Commission on Human Rights resolution 1999/36. United Nations Economic and Social Council, 11 February. www.unhchr.ch/Huridocta/Huridoca.nsf/Testframe/5c111c8bbfc8455d802 568b9004baofc?
Kelly, T. (1998) *Information Strategy*, 4 March. Internal memo from the Director of Communications leaked to the Democratic Unionist Party.
Kiberd, D. (ed.) (1999) *Media in Ireland: the search for ethical journalism*, Dublin: Open Air.
Kirby, S. (1999) 'Selling the Good Friday Agreement: A Public Relations Perspective', unpublished dissertation for MSc in Public Relations,University of Stirling.
Lago, R. (1998) 'Interviewing Sinn Féin under the New Political Environment: a comparative analysis of interviews with Sinn Féin on British Television' in *Media, Culture and Society*, 20 (4): 687–95.

Lewis, R. (1999) *Fishers of Men*, London: Hodder and Stoughton.

McGartland, M. (1998) *Fifty Dead Men Walking*, London: Blake Publishing.

McGartland, M. (1999) *Dead Man Running*, Edinburgh: Mainstream.

McKittrick, David (1993) 'Disbelief in Britain's words', *Independent on Sunday*, 5 December: 6.

Miller, David (1994) *Don't Mention the War: Northern Ireland, Propaganda and the Media*, London: Pluto.

Miller, David (1995a) 'The reel crisis in Ireland', *New Statesman and Society*, 4 August: 31–2.

Miller, David (1995b) 'The media and Northern Ireland: Censorship, information management and the broadcasting ban', in Greg Philo (ed.) *The Glasgow Media Group Reader, Volume II*, London: Routledge.

Miller, David and McLaughlin, Greg (1996) 'Reporting the peace in Ireland' in Rolston, Bill and Miller, David (ed.) *War and Words: The Northern Ireland Media Reader*, Belfast: Beyond the Pale. Miller, David (1997) 'Manipulating the message', *Irish News*, 8 January: 10.

Miller, David (1998) 'Colonialism and Academic Representations of the Troubles', in Miller, David (ed.) *Rethinking Northern Ireland: Colonialism, Power and Ideology*, London: Longman.

Mullin, J. (2000) 'Journalist faces "dirty tricks" arrest', *The Guardian*, 16 May: 6.

Northern Ireland Office (1997) *Review of Information Services in Northern Ireland*, November, Belfast: NIO.

Norton-Taylor, R. (2000) 'Secrets and spies', *The Guardian*, 18 May: 21.

O'Callaghan, S. (1999) *The Informer*, London: Corgi.

O'Toole, M. (1997) 'Anatomy of a campaign of smear and innuendo', *Irish News*, 6 January.

Ritchie, M. (2000) 'The media must play its part in peace', *Irish News*, 16 May.

Rolston, B. (1996) *Turning the Page without Closing the Book*, Belfast: Beyond the Pale.

Stanfield, M. (1999) 'File under "w"', *Fortnight* 377, March.

Sunday Times (1999) 'Court gag protects army dirty tricks unit', 28 November.

Walker, G. (1995) 'BBC to rule on harassment claim', *Belfast Telegraph*, 11 May.

Cleraun Media Conferences

The chapters in this volume are based on papers delivered to the Eighth Cleraun Media Conference held in Dublin on 12–13 February 2000. The title of the conference was 'Media in Ireland: ethical issues in broadcasting'. The contribution of those who chaired the conference sessions is gratefully acknowledged. They were:

RICHARD BRUTON TD
Former Minister for Enterprise and Employment

PAUL CULLEN
Development Correspondent, *Irish Times*

JOHN EGAN
Reporter/Presenter, *The World Tonight*, BBC Radio 4, London

MICHAEL FOLEY
Senior Lecturer in journalism, Dublin Institute of Technology, and media commentator

CAIMIN JONES
Media consultant and former Managing Director, Clare FM

JOHN LONERGAN
Governor, Mountjoy Prison

DR MARTIN MANSERGH
Special Adviser to the Taoiseach

MARK O'CONNELL
Political Correspondent, *Sunday Business Post*

BOB QUINN
Independent film producer, member of Aosdána, and former member of the RTE Authority

Also gratefully acknowledged is the help received from André Raynouard and Martine Moreau of the French Embassy in Dublin, from RTE, and from the British Council.

Previous Cleraun Media Conferences have looked at a broad range of topics including:

- the role of media practitioners in society
- public service broadcasting and democracy
- the dangers posed by new media monopolies
- proposals to create a greater diversity in media
- ethical issues in news reporting, coverage of conflict, and advertising
- the media on terrorism, violence and crime
- the role of the media in the Northern Ireland peace process
- the use of broadcasting bans by government
- Church-media relations

- opening access to the airwaves and community radio
- investigative journalism
- regional versus national press
- media education
- ethical standards in the US, British and French media
- ideas on a philosophical foundation for media ethics
- Irish daily newspaper coverage of the refugee issue
- the responsibilities of media owners
- standards and litigation
- codes of conduct
- the newspaper ombudsman
- leaks to the media

Papers based on previous Cleraun Media Conferences were also published by Open Air:

- *Media in Ireland: the search for diversity* (ISBN 1-85182-315-8), now in its second printing, was launched by Micheál Martin TD, Minister of Education, in 1997 (see page 138).

- *Media in Ireland: the search for ethical journalism* (ISBN 1-85182-509-6) was launched by Liz O'Donnell TD, Minister of State for Foreign Affairs, in 1999 (see page 137).

The conferences are held in Cleraun at 90 Foster Avenue, Mount Merrion, Co. Dublin—a study centre and hall of residence for third level students which is an apostolic undertaking of Opus Dei, a prelature of the Catholic Church.

Notes on contributors

Michael Beattie produced Ulster Television's weekly current affairs programme *Insight* and is now an independent film producer. He spent ten years in UTV's senior management, as Head of News and Current Affairs, and as Assistant Programme Controller. His documentaries have won many awards at home and abroad.

Joe Duffy presents the daily national phone-in programme *Liveline* on RTE Radio 1. He was a producer on many programmes, including *The Gay Byrne Show*.

Dr Thierry Garcin is a producer at France-Culture, Radio-France, and a foreign and defence policy journalist. He is also a professor at the École des Hautes Études Internationales and at the École Supérieure de Journalisme in Paris, and has published widely.

Dr Patrick Gorevan is a priest of the Opus Dei prelature and chaplain to Rosemont Park School in Dublin. He has published on phenomenology and emotional theory, and teaches philosophy. He is joint-editor of the monthly magazine *Position Papers*.

Ursula Halligan is the political editor of TV3 and was TV Journalist of the Year in 2000. She has worked on RTE TV's current affairs programme *Primetime*, with the *Sunday Times*, the *Sunday Tribune* and *Magill* magazine.

William Hunt is an American financial consultant, now based in Ireland, who has worked in Greece and the Middle East.

Damien Kiberd was until recently editor of the *Sunday Business Post*. He was editor of *Media in Ireland: the search for ethical journalism* and *Media in Ireland: the search for diversity*, both published by Open Air.

George Lee is economics editor of RTE. In 1998, together with RTE's special correspondent Charlie Bird, he wrote *Breaking the Bank: how the NIB scandal was exposed* (Blackwater), which detailed how they broke the story of National Irish Bank's offshore financial scheme, which earned both journalists the overall prize in the 1998 National Media Awards.

David Miller is a lecturer in media studies at Stirling University in Scotland and a member of its Media Research Institute. His books include *Don't Mention the War: Northern Ireland, propaganda and the media* (Pluto, 1994) and he was editor of *War and Words: the Northern Ireland media reader* (Beyond the Pale, 1996, with Bill Rolston) and *Rethinking Northern Ireland: culture, ideology and colonialism* (Longman, 1998).

Adrian Moynes is Special Assistant to the Director-General of RTE. His special interest is broadcasting policy. He has worked with RTE for twenty years, as a producer in TV and radio, as head of programmes for young people, and as head of schedule planning.

Breda O'Brien is a columnist with the *Irish Times*, a teacher at a secondary school for girls in Dublin, and a mother of four children under eight.

Maggie O'Kane is a special correspondent on foreign affairs with *The Guardian* and a TV and radio broadcaster. Her awards include British Journalist of the Year, Joint Amnesty International Foreign Correspondent of the Year, British Television Society: Best Documentary of the Year, and James Cameron Memorial Trust Award for Journalism. Her TV documentaries include *The Face of Debt* (Channel 4), *Haiti—the bad boys of Port au Prince* (BBC), *The Gulf War: how to tell lies and win wars* (Channel 4), *The Puppet Master of the Balkans* (BBC). Her radio documentaries include *The Last Women Left Alive: missing in action in Vietnam* (BBC Radio 4).

Index

Media in Ireland
The Search for Ethical Journalism
Damien Kiberd, Editor

CONTENTS

'Irish journalism needs to do some ethical thinking, and *The Search for Ethical Journalism*, the outcome of the Seventh Cleraun Media Conference, does a good job at opening up the issues' David Quin, *Irish Communications Review*, 8 (2000).

'The question of ethics within journalism has never been more topical. This collection of essays enters the debate, with eight prominent journalists and academics hammering out the case for a system of professional ethics' Gerard McCann, *Global Issues*, Belfast, February 2000.

'This book emphasises that ethics in journalism goes way beyond the hoary issues of accuracy and privacy. It will enlighten all who read it' Minister of State Liz O'Donnell TD at the launch of the book in the National Library of Ireland.

Open Air 128pp ISBN 1-85182-509-6 pbk €14.95 (1999)

Media in Ireland
The Search for Diversity
Damien Kiberd, Editor

CONTENTS

'Much else in this book should cause journalists and editors to blush. It is more important, however, that they find a way of acknowledging the stimulation and responding to the arguments' Brian Trench, *Sunday Tribune*.

'This is a well-written and readable work. Joanna Bogle's perspective on Church-media relations should be compulsory reading for every news editor in the country' Michael Breen, *Irish Catholic*.

'The impressive range of contributors to this book comprehensively outlines the complexity of an issue which is often superficially presented as being about ownership. It does not simply examine the current state of the Irish media, it looks beyond this and outlines ways in which a true diversity can be developed and maintained' Minister Micheál Martin TD at the launch of the book in the National Library of Ireland.

Open Air 96pp ISBN 1-85182-315-8 pbk €14.95 (1997, reprinted 1998)